THE
Green
MILLIONAIRE

A PRACTICAL GUIDE TO ACHIEVING REAL WEALTH
WHILE HELPING TO SAVE THE PLANET

NIGEL J. WILLIAMS

1-4392-2212-6

9781439222126

The Green Millionaire
Copyright © 2009 Nigel Williams
All rights reserved
Published in the US by Green Marble, LLC
Printed in the US

Cover Design by Myra Ferrie

Photos: Photos.com
First Edition

For my wife Ivy,
daughter Sean, and
son Oliver and my partner
Scott who have been with me
on this enlightening journey.

Thank you.

"We shall require a substantially new manner of thinking if humanity is to survive."

Albert Einstein, 1954

Contents

Don't

Panic.

When I first started working on this book, the world was a different place. Now, as I write this, the economic news has worsened. Headlines tell us we are heading into the worst financial times in decades.

So how can I say "don't panic?"

Because there are concrete steps we can take to get through this. I am not saying you won't have difficult choices to make over the next few years, but as individuals we will emerge stronger financially, as a nation we will emerge stronger economically, and as a global community we will emerge stronger environmentally.

We must start by asking ourselves tough but essential questions. Do we really need our super-sized gas guzzlers, our huge houses, our lavish vacations, and our new gadgets and appliances? I hope that by asking such questions that the scales will drop from our eyes and we will see that the answers are an emphatic No! Not only do we not need these things, but shedding our perceived dependence upon them is much easier than we'd ever think.

In fact, it's simple. And my family and I are much happier today for taking control of these programmed impulses than we've ever been before.

Our economic situation is forcing us to be green: We are using less gas, buying fewer consumer goods, and watching the pennies. Is that so bad? It's what our parents did.

Anyone facing financial difficulties right now will find this book helpful; it will alter your perspective by presenting a monetary incentive to question your assumptions. You win twice. You will see that as you start to notice the differences that green choices make in your life, you will be motivated to do more.

There is more to a "green" lifestyle than simply saving the planet. And there is more to a "millionaire" lifestyle than just having cash in the bank. The true value of each lies in the freedom they impart to the individual.

This book is about attaining those freedoms—and something far greater—by discovering where these interests overlap.

I am going to show you how to reclaim your sense of possibility about life by making a few simple changes.

Introducing the Three Steps
to Becoming a
Green
Millionaire.

Attention.

The first step is to begin paying attention to the routine, daily behavior that fails to benefit the environment or increase your family's finances.

Action.

This book is full of simple solutions to common household financial problems. But acting on them is the key. Results proceed from action, so please take advantage of the tools provided. Whenever you see this symbol you can log on to www.TheGreenMillionaire.com to find out more.

Accumulation.

This is where it gets fun. Use The Green Millionaire workbook provided to discover your "Green Savings" and fuel your financial freedom. You'll find that saving even a tiny amount each day will quickly add up to become significant wealth.

What Is a "GREEN MILLIONAIRE"?

A Green Millionaire is someone who recognizes that **"going green"** means investing in the future as well as enjoying life today. With the simple ideas outlined in this book, you'll be amazed how you will feel more in control of your finances today, while knowing that you will have real wealth and independence in the future.

All this by doing small things each day, and by starting to think and act like a millionaire.

Congratulations.
You're on your way to becoming the next GREEN MILLIONAIRE.

Congratulations on buying this book. And on opening it. And on actually starting to read it.

That puts you on the first step toward becoming a Green Millionaire.

A Green Millionaire is someone who enjoys the finer things in life. He or she also understands that our actions as individuals have a collective effect on the planet, and that by conserving the things we buy we can generate ourselves at least a million dollars.

Green Millionaires are not cheap, but rather they are smart. And Green Millionaires are not misers—they are generous with their time and resources.

Being a Green Millionaire means you're aware of what you're consuming.

All you need to do to become a Green Millionaire is to start thinking like one. Once you've read this book you'll walk around with your Green Millionaire glasses on, seeing opportunities to increase your wealth everywhere.

You will realize that every ungreen choice you make costs you money. That even the most unconscious, habitual daily choices can erode your nest egg. And that over the next twenty years, every dollar you're able to put into your bank account each year will amount to another $63 toward your retirement.

Green Millionaires are considered cool by their friends and co-workers, who see them as doing the right thing but in their own way.

On a personal note, I started this project as a way to address the problem of global warming. It seemed to me that if we stopped doing the things that caused the problem, then the problem would be solved. Simple! Or so I thought.

The environment is not such an easy problem to isolate; there are many interconnected parts . For example, businesses succeed because they follow their mandate of supplying what we as consumers demand.

But as we let market forces take more control of our lives, the need for businesses to remain the low-price leader becomes evermore important to them.

This can lead to degraded manufacturing standards designed to keep the ever-demanding bulls on Wall Street from the boardroom door (while likely shielding us from questionable manufacturing processes). But now the bull has come around to stick us: Those of us not in the boardroom find ourselves working for lower wages inside companies that struggle for profits. And we come to discover that, through this unfortunate cycle, we have priced ourselves right out of the market for those products that we had originally demanded.

Lower profits for business. Lower wages for workers. Nobody is winning.

I've envisioned this book to be the first small step in taking back our finances, our environment, and our lives.

How To Turn
WATER Into WEALTH.

It's amazing that the actions we so innocently take on a daily basis can have such a huge negative effect upon our future wealth, and upon the future of the planet.

Many books have been written on the subject of going green, which is both good and bad. Good because it raises awareness that we must do something, and bad because, frankly, it paralyzes us about doing anything at all. It's like going to the gym and seeing all the exercise equipment. We know it will do us good, but where to start? And will those one or two machines really make a difference?

That's where I come in. I want to be your personal trainer of green. I will vet the various green options and give you my honest opinion about them. I will strongly suggest that you heed the advice given here. I am not going to suggest any crazy stuff like turning up the air conditioning thermostat during the hot summer months and walking around the house naked, although perhaps that's never a bad idea when certain in-laws come to visit.

The things I will suggest are simple steps that anyone can take. After all, greenness is not something you a can attain overnight. It is a journey as well as a destination. And as your buying habits change, so will the products people offer. Look at lite beer or hybrid cars. These products exist today as direct responses to consumer wishes. You really have more power over big companies than you think.

You will see a chart like this that shows how much you'll save, how easy a given action is to perform, and how much the planet benefits. This is useful because it will allow you to make some quick decisions on what you are willing to change.

Throughout the book you will see charts like this that show how easy it is to become a Green Millionaire. Here, for example, are some simple steps you can take to eliminate bottled water in favor of filtered drinking water.

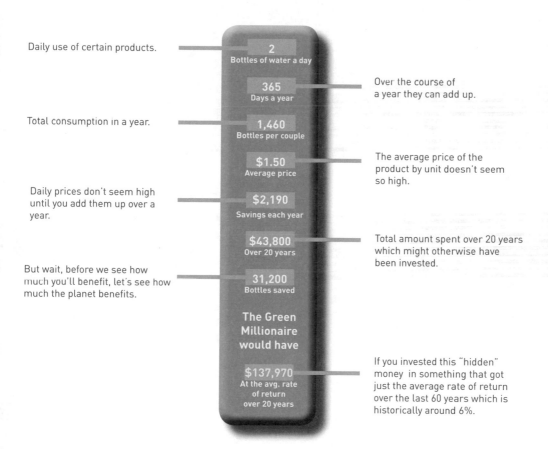

Daily use of certain products.

2
Bottles of water a day

Over the course of a year they can add up.

365
Days a year

Total consumption in a year.

1,460
Bottles per couple

The average price of the product by unit doesn't seem so high.

$1.50
Average price

Daily prices don't seem high until you add them up over a year.

$2,190
Savings each year

$43,800
Over 20 years

Total amount spent over 20 years which might otherwise have been invested.

But wait, before we see how much you'll benefit, let's see how much the planet benefits.

31,200
Bottles saved

The Green Millionaire would have

$137,970
At the avg. rate of return over 20 years

If you invested this "hidden" money in something that got just the average rate of return over the last 60 years which is historically around 6%.

We All Know We Should Do Something
About The Environment,
BUT WHAT?

We've seen the movies the TV shows
telling us that we need to do something about
global warming and the climate crisis. But where
do we begin? Do we shut off all the amazing
new devices we're now addicted to and have
grown to love? The use of electrical energy has
gone up exponentially over the last 60 years,
with no end in sight. If we're not prepared to
turn off our gadgets, then where do we find the
energy necessary to use them?

This book is not going to be another book to
make you feel bad about your lifestyle. This
book is to encourage you to liberate yourself
from being owned by your things rather than the
other way around.

I am not advocating sacrifice. Far from it. I
just want you to look at another way of buying
products. One that doesn't cost you any more
money. In fact, the tips in this book will actually
save you money—some in the short term, but
most in the long term. Imagine locking in your
electric bill for 25 years, or never having to pay
for gas. All of these options are real, and con-
tained in this book.

Consider that the average family works for two
solid months a year to pay for each car they
drive.

Does going green mean going without?

Witness the Tesla car. This car can out-perform a Lamborghini and costs about $.05 a mile. The engine weighs only 110 lbs. and reaches speeds over 120 mph. All it requires is a plug in the wall.

The PACIFIC Ocean Gyres.

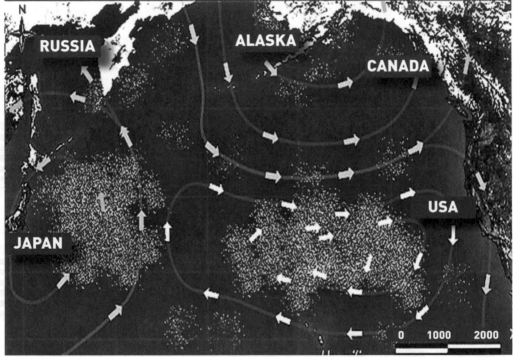

There are "land masses" in most of our major oceans that are made up of plastic particles, billions of tons of plastic, that just go around and around in what's called a "gyre."

These particles grind against each other and become smaller pieces that are eaten by fish and other marine life. Guess who eats the fish?

FACT: Plastic does not biodegrade like most materials. After your 12-ounces of water is gone, the plastic from that bottle will still be around for several hundred years!

If you consider that the United States alone disposes of over 23 billion empty plastic bottles each year...well, you begin to get the horrific picture.

FACT: Plastic photodegrades with exposure to sunlight. Even so, it will still take a thousand years to reduce the plastic to molecular dust.

Algalita Marina Research Foundation photo by Matt Cramer

What's the problem with tons of plastic garbage floating hundreds of miles from land and visible animal life? Plenty.

Far from being devoid of animal life, deep-ocean surfaces are like vast cradles for the microscopic plant and animal life that are at the base of the food chain. This is where phytoplankton (microscopic plants) is produced in abundance, which feeds the zooplankton (tiny animal organisms) that feed the smaller fish, that feed the larger fish, that feed us!

Plastics that break down into tiny pellets act like sponges that absorb toxic chemicals that are not water soluble. These pellets are eaten by fish and the chemicals are absorbed into their flesh. The plastic toxins have now entered our food chain.

Albatross feed on fish by scooping them out of the water., Unfortunately, they can't distinguish plastic from fish.

Photo courtesy Dino Ferri, Audubon Institute

Just one example of what happens to the plastic we throw away. This turtle has lived with plastic caught around its shell since it was young.

When we eat the fish, the toxins are then absorbed into our flesh.

These floating masses of toxic waste are growing every day, and they're moving. They pollute beaches and kill hundreds of thousands of aquatic, air, and land animals each year.

They say a picture is worth a thousand words. See more on the Great Pacific Garbage Patch: Wikipedia.com

Photo: Cynthia Vanderlip

Why do we consumers prefer water that
..... comes in bottled containers over water
we can get from our home tap?

..... Very clever advertising.

H₂Ohhhh!

Without it we humans would not survive more than a few days. It's a life essential that normally rains down on us from the heavens in glorious abundance, for free!

So it's quite bewildering to realize that we have taken something so basic and pure as water and transformed it into a complex and expensive commodity. It belies common sense.

A simple glass of water. Most would agree it's a rare sight to see these days. More common is the sight of bottled water. Everywhere.

These harmless-looking beverages have become the world's multi-billion-dollar-a-year obsession.

Wholesale dollar sales of bottled water exceeded $12 billion in the U.S. in 2007. And nine times out of ten that bottle is made up of single-use plastic.

Over 30 billion empty soda and water bottles are produced each and every year in the U.S.

Less than 20% of plastic bottles are recycled. Most end up in landfills, or floating out in the middle of our oceans.

Even so, a lot of people might be asking, "How do I know what's in my tap water?" And, "Doesn't bottled water just taste better?"

With bottled mineral water, the taste may or may not be detectable. But mineral water is not regulated and therefore the quality can never be guaranteed from bottle to bottle.

On the other hand, most bottled water sold today is not mineral water but just tap water.

What's the green solution?
Filter your own water and fill up your own re-useable water bottle.

Everyone knows this one, right? Everyone knows, but as evidenced by U.S. annual bottled-water consumption, not everyone is convinced that it's worth doing.

Consider this:
Each and every person buying just one bottled water a day can save at least $750 a year by drinking filtered water from his or her own re-useable water bottle.

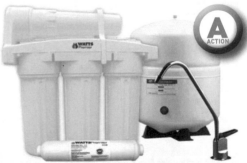

You could do what I do and have a reverse osmosis system under your sink. It makes all your food taste better.

$ $ $ Involved

2	Bottles of water a day
365	Days a year
1,460	Bottles per couple
$1.50	Average price
$2,190	Savings each year
$43,800	Over 20 years
31,200	Bottles saved

The Green Millionaire would have

$137,970
At the avg. rate of return over 20 years

Bottled water is 10,000 times more expensive than tap water.

How about a simple dispenser in the fridge that has a filter that you fill up with regular tap water? One filter can replace hundreds of water bottles.

Or if you are on the go, take a personal filtration system with you. This ingenious bottle has a filter right inside it, and can replace 1,110 water bottles.

There are so many easy and fun ways to avoid using plastic bottles.

$	No-Brainer	🌐🌐🌐🌐

20

Food, Glorious
FOOD

The average U.S. household spends $800 a year on food that ends up being thrown away. What's more, producing, transporting, and consuming food is responsible for nearly a third of each individual's contribution to climate change.

Making a few simple changes to the way you shop for food can save hundreds of dollars on your shopping bill and slim down your carbon footprint.

1. Plan your meals.
Planning your meals in advance of your weekly shop is one of the most effective ways you can reduce the food you waste. Making a shopping list of the things you need for those meals, and trying to stick to it, means you're less likely to end up with items you won't use.

2. Know what you've got.
Checking your fridge, freezer and store cupboard so you don't shop for things you already have will save you money. It's a good idea to have a quick look when you're making your shopping list.

3. Think about portion sizes.
When buying food, consider how many people will be eating and what size portions they are likely to eat. There are many useful tools available to measure portions, from a tablespoon to a spaghetti measurer, that you might want to think about investing in. This could help reduce the amount of food you need to buy—and the amount left on the plates at the end of a meal.

4. Buy seasonal food.
Eating seasonal food can help tackle climate change—that's because it sometimes requires less energy to produce than food grown out of season or stored for long periods of time. Challenge yourself to cook a few meals using fruit, vegetables, meat, and fish that are

Over $150 billion of food is thrown away every year in this country. We could feed the planet just in the food we waste.

in season.

5. Plan your trip to the store.

By planning what you need to buy in advance, you can cut down on the number of trips you make to the supermarket. Making fewer food shopping trips by car, or using other forms of transport instead, will help cut emissions and could even save you money.

6. And when you're finished...

If you can't reuse your food, compost it. You can get a kitchen composter, Home composting diverts waste from landfill, saving on climate change emissions—and it can also provide a cheap compost for the garden.

$ Easy

Your daily coffee costs you $1,250 a year.

It costs the planet a lot more.

The $2,700 Coffee Habit.

1
Coffee a day
per person

730
Coffees a year
per couple

$3
Average per
serving

$2,190
Savings a year

$43,800
Over 20 Years

**The Green
Millionaire
would have**

$137,970
At the avg. rate
of return over
20 years

Imagine the waste of 40 million paper cups a day. It would constitute a wall as wide as a city block and 50 stories high. Every day.

Coffee. I can't start my day without it. Not sure why I do it, but you will see me waiting for 10 minutes in line for a "Grande Soy Decaf Cappuccino" in the morning and after lunch. Or I used to, that is, until I got an amazing cappuccino maker at home. I think it paid for itself in a month. If I made one for each coffee-drinking member of our family every day, it would be like saving $12 a day.

I'm not sure why we started buying these mocha-frappa lattes, but it has certainly become a big business.

I was recently driving down the street and saw two coffee stores with the familiar green mermaid logo located opposite one another!

Funnily enough, about the only country that does not host the big multinational green mermaid is Italy, the true home of the espresso. And the espresso maker.

Make your own cappuccinos.

This could be the most effective tip to propel you to Green Millionaire status quickly.

Get a cappuccino machine for your home or office. Or get your company to buy one. (Tell them it will improve productivity.) Skip the coffee line on the way to work and make something that is better-tasting and way better on your wallet.

Plus, you won't need those plastic stirrers or plastic lids or carrying cases that just get thrown away. Better yet, use your favorite travel mug. You can buy the exact same beans they use at many different stores.

My big tip is to get a good grinder. That will make all the difference.

You will make friends at work.

I purchased a deluxe machine for work a few years back and would go in the kitchen and start frothing (coffee-making, that is). People would strike up a conversation and I would make them a cup.

So how is this so green?

Just imagine the waste of 300 million people drinking coffee every day.

Making your own coffee with simple capsules in a few seconds can save you thousands a year.

$ $ $	Easy	

Use your own thermos mug. It'll keep your coffee warmer and eliminate a lot of waste. Or even use a poreclain cup, which looks just like a paper cup but makes the coffee taste better.

$ $ $	Easy	

26

Imagine Carrying Home 60,000 Cans of Soda.

2 Sodas a day per person
2,920 Soda beverages a year per Family
$0.75 Average per serving
$2,190 Savings a year
$43,800 Over 20 Years
The Green Millionaire would have
$137,970 At the avg. rate of return over 20 years

That's how many servings of soda the average family will consume over the next 20 years. That's 10 thousand six-packs. And that is just an average family; many people drink way more than that. It makes me tired just thinking about it.

Americans drink more than 13 billion gallons of soda and seltzer each year. That's almost 50 gallons, or about 600 cans for every adult and child in the United States. According to the Environmental Protection Agency, that adds over three billion cubic feet of trash to our landfills and recycling facilities every year.

Fortunately, there is a great solution to our thirst for soda: a home soda fountain. Invented in 1903 in England, this used to be a luxury item for the elite, and sold strictly to the upper classes, including the royal family.

It was especially popular when I was a kid growing up in England. Now it's affordable for everyone.

It's mind-blowing. Every man, woman, and child in the U.S. drinks 50 gallons per person and 200 gallons per family. Over 20 years, that's 4,000 gallons . And that's just if you are average.

The Green Millionaire has found this product and tells you where you can get it.

You'll enjoy freshly made, great-tasting seltzer and soda in just seconds. And you'll be helping our environment by drastically reducing waste from store-bought cans and bottles.

A family of four can slash their consumption of soft-drink-related packaging by over 90% simply by using a soda maker. That's a whole lot of cans and bottles that won't end up polluting our environment.

A typical American will toss away over 1,500 aluminum cans, and hundreds of plastic two-liter bottles over three years, while a home soda maker will use just one or two re-usable carbonating bottles.

Pretty much any flavor you can imagine is available.

The other great thing about these home soda-fountain systems is that they don't use the high-fructose corn syrups that many believe are responsible for a multitude of health problems in our youth, including obesity and diabetes.

They also contain up to one-third the calories and carbs of traditional sodas.

Meaning that you'll have a healthier you and a healthier planet.

- *No batteries or electricity*
- *Reduces energy used to manufacture bottles and cans*
- *Reduces gas and pollution from shipping packaged beverages*

$ $ $ **Easy**

One Soda Club machine can make all your favorite drinks for five cents a glass. And no waste.

How to Keep Your COOL at Night.

$200 Avg. electric bill
7° Increase in thermostat
$38 Monthly savings
$456 Savings each year
$9,120 Over 20 years
The Green Millionaire would have
$28,728 At the avg. rate of return over 20 years

The ability to control the temperature of your house? What a wonderful invention. Although it allows us to tolerate 100-degree weather, it comes at a price.

Air conditioning accounts for 45% of the average home's energy budget.

So how can we reduce this?

One way to start saving energy and reduce your A/C bill would be to raise your thermostat a few degrees. Raising your temperature at night will reduce your energy consumption dramatically. If you're like me, though, that's not an option. I come from England and I'm used to cool weather, and have difficulty sleeping in any temperature over 70 degrees.

Here's a solution that thinks small: Why not just cool you? At night you don't move around the house anyway, so why not make a micro-climate in your bed, under your sheets? The human body has a great way of cooling itself by producing sweat from sweat glands. And the circulation of air will reduce the surface temperature up to

Turn your thermostat up 8-10 degrees at night with this cool device.

20 degrees. So far, so good. But if you are in bed it is difficult to get air flowing around you.

Don't cool your whole house, just cool you.

The Bedfan personal cooling system provides the cool relief you need in order to raise your thermostat by as much as eight degrees and still remain comfortable over a short period of time. This small amount of change in your thermostat setting will allow you to start saving energy and lower your electric bill tonight.

For every degree the thermostat is raised, 4% to 8% can be saved on cooling costs. The personal cooling system costs only nickels per month to operate and can pay for itself in just a

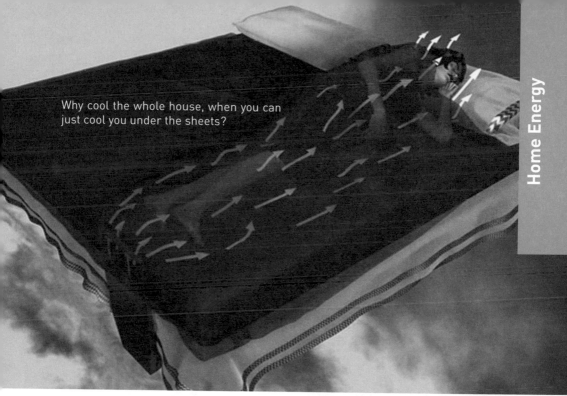

Why cool the whole house, when you can just cool you under the sheets?

few months, sometimes weeks. Also, it can work on one side of the bed, leaving the other side unaffected, which in many families is a blessing, as people often can't agree on the right thermostat setting at night.

How to avoid being a hot head.

If you're like me you like a cool pillow. There is now an invention called the "Chillow" that's a godsend to those wanting to sleep on a cool pillow all night. Just put it in the fridge and then insert it in your pillow. *Voila!* you have a cool pillow all night. And think of the money you'll save not blasting your A/C all night cooling the whole house when you could just be cooling you.

Imagine the savings to the environment by keeping your cool.

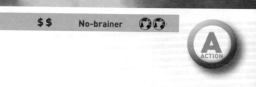

Keep your pillow cool all night with the "Chillow." No more turning the pillow over to find the coolest side.

You Give Electricity Back To the Power Companies For FREE.

This gray box can save you thousands of dollars and all your appliances will work just as well after you install it. This is truly the lazy man's way of protecting the environment while making major savings.

Did you know that you give back as much as 25% of your electricity to the power companies?

How to reduce your utility bill.
In your house there are appliances, such as ceiling fans, dishwashers, pool pumps, washing machines—in fact, anything with a motor. These motors store electrical power in order to function, but when they have done with the power they return it to the power grid. Your meter is not set up to show power going out, so you never know how much stored energy you're giving back. But kiss it good-bye.

What if you could save that energy and re-use it in the house? That could save you and the environment a lot of money.

There is a simple gray box you can install yourself that will do just this. All it does is save the power from being returned so that you can re-use it.

This device will pay for itself in six months.

$ $ $ Involved

Why doesn't everyone know about this? Well, we've been paying very low rates for a long time—two to four cents a kilowatt. But that figure has shot up to as much as 22 cents, even 33 cents in Hawaii. Consumption awareness is good for the environment because it means we are using less energy these days. But it's not been great for our budgets, which are still affected by the invisible flow of energy surging back to the utility company. That's where this device comes in.

This is truly the lazy man's way of protecting the environment while making major savings.

Any appliance that has a motor will store energy (inductive load) and send it back to the grid. This can account for 20% of your entire electric bill. Just wasted power.

The Earth gets enough sun
in just one day to give us all the
energy we need for **300** years.

Get $30,000
Solar Panels Installed FREE.

$140
Avg. monthly
electric bill

$1,680
Annual savings

$33,600
Over 20 years

**The Green
Millionaire
would have**

$105,840
At the avg. rate
of return
over 20 years

The U.S. Energy Information Administration forecast that electricity prices will climb an average of 9.8% in 2009.

Natural gas has been increasing at an alarming rate.

You can get $25,000 worth of solar panels installed and maintained for free, saving you 20% right now on your electric bill, while locking in that rate for the next 25 years. Even if you move.

If you had done this 10 or 20 years ago, imagine how low your power bills would be today. But there's still time to make a difference. Take action now and you will lock in your rates until 2033, while others will be paying thousands of dollars per month. And here's the best part: Imagine how much greenhouse gas you'll keep from seeping into the environment over that time. A Green Millionaire knows how to save not only the planet but his own wallet. And you won't have to feel guilty about leaving lights on because you won't be burning coal or harming the environment in any way.

Remember, this COSTS YOU NOTHING.

$ $ $ $ Involved   ✿✿✿✿

Become your own power station by selling your excess solar power back to the utility company. **WOW!**

Have your roof make you Money

Did you know that you can power your home for free? You can!! Once you go solar, it's likely that you won't have to pay a dime to run your A/C or keep the lights on. What's more, you don't have to worry about wasting precious energy – the sun is a renewable resource!! Take green-leader Larry Hagman. He powers his own and 5 of his neighbors homes with his solar array!!

Sell your Energy back to the Utility Company

Yes!! You can make money by going solar. In fact, once you have your solar system installed, your local utility company will pay you the market price for any excess energy you are creating. But how does it work? Basically, when you create excess energy, the meter spins backwards. The utility company then records this surplus and gives you money for it. Easy!!

Although every utility program is different, there is definitely money to be made here. In some programs for example, the utility company will send the customers a monthly bill. If there is negative energy consumption, it is credited to your account and paid (at market rate) at the end of the year. Of course you get the satisfaction of making money and saving the environment. It's a win win situation.

The Government Will Give You Money

Believe it or not, the Government will give you money to go solar. No matter what state you live in, whether you own a home or a business, whether you're building a house or already own one, there are state and federal incentives, rebates, and giveaways available to you.

So how do you find them? The first thing to do is to go to www.dsireusa.org and click on your state. There you'll find that you can search for incentives for businesses and residences provided by both state and federal agencies.

There are hundreds and hundreds of programs available!! Did you know, for example, that there is 3.2 billion dollars available for solar energy projects in California alone? And this is regardless of whether you own a residence or a business.

Can't Buy? Why Not Rent?

Did you know that you can rent your solar equipment? New programs available today allow homeowners to rent solar equipment with little or no investment. What's more, companies will install and maintain your equipment for you – even if you move. As an added benefit, most solar rental companies offer customers a reduced per-kilowatt fee at a price which is "locked in" for several years. Of course, you'll want to do your research. There are hundreds of companies out there who specialize in providing solar systems for individuals who can't or don't want to buy. Look around to see what works best for you.

$ $ $ $ Involved

Money is Leaking Out of Your
HOUSE.

Visualize your money seeping out your attic roof, or through the cracks around your doors and windows. We are talking about nearly $500 a year for the average house. And as energy costs keep going up, that number will only increase. Imagine the benefit to the environment if all of us were able to reduce our electricity consumption by 20%? You can find good information about this at www.energystar.gov.

Weather-stripping.

Did you know that airsealing your home and adding insulation in your attic, floor, and basement can save you up to 20% off heating and cooling costs (or around 10% of total energy costs)? It can!! And it's easy!!

Sealing leaks.

Most people discover that it's rather easy to find the most obvious of air leaks in their homes: such as those around doors and windows.

That said, there are other sources of wasted energy that may need your attention. Holes in basements, attics, and crawl spaces can be sealed with weather-stripping, caulk, or spray-foam. Whichever method you choose, you can be sure that costly energy bills and uncomfortable drafts will be reduced significantly.

Keep in mind that there is a certain amount of fresh air that is necessary for good health. Make sure to have a heating-and-cooling technician inspect appliances such as water heaters, dryers, and oil or gas fired furnaces following completion of your home-sealing projects.

Adding insulation.

Adding Insulation is a great way to save money and energy. Keeping your home warm in the winter and cool in the summer, there are several common types of insulating materials such as cellulose, spray foam, batt and blown fiberglass, and rigid foam board. For hotter climates, many find that reflective insulation, or radiant barrier, is the optimal insulation to keep out the heat.

The first place to look, when considering insulation, is right above you in your attic. If your attic floor is uncovered, you can be sure that insulation will help decrease costs and increase comfort. Prior to insulation, make sure that all air leaks are sealed as this guarantees the greatest efficiency.

Keep in mind that insulation is measured by its ability to resist the flow of heat. This is called the R-Value. Depending upon your area of the country, and whether you are seeking to insulate a wall, basement, crawlspace, or attic, different R-Values are recommended. Since you want to get the most out of your insulation, make sure to do your research prior to beginning your project.

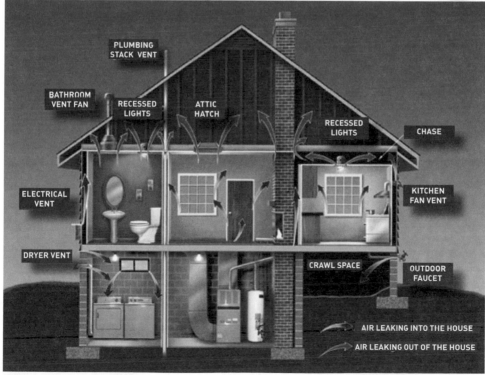

$ $ $ Involved

Are You Full of
HOT AIR?

How can the sun cool your hot attic space and save you money?

When the temperature outside is 100° the temperature in your attic can be in excess of 150°. It becomes like an oven. The small, passive roof vents are not great at dissipating this heat. Sometimes they don't even move. This lets heat back into your living spaces, even with insulation, sending temperatures and cooling bills through the roof.

Our roof keeps the house hot even at night when it's cool outside. Also, in my house we have moisture that gets trapped, causing thousands of dollars of sheet rock and other damage to the house. This moisture promotes the growth of mold and mildew.

Installing a solar attic fan can save the homeowner money in two ways. First, it will reduce your heating and cooling costs in the short term. Second, it will increase the life of your roof and reduce the need for repairs due to moisture, which can otherwise add up to thousands of dollars. We didn't know what was causing our crumbling ceilings—we thought it was a leaking roof. We replaced the roof and all the ceilings, but guess what? A few months later the problem came back. We would have saved over 10 thousand dollars by having this installed earlier.

The roof receives direct sunlight and heat begins building up in the attic space. Moisture also enters the attic space from activities such as bathing, cooking, and laundering. If you don't remove this heat and moisture, damage can occur, such as mold and dry rot.

As the attic space overheats, the underside of the shingles will heat up. This causes unnecessary wear-and-tear on your shingles. Your 25-year roof may only last you only 10 years.

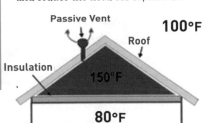

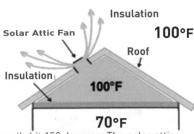

When it's 100 degrees outside a normal attic could easily hit 150 degrees. The solar attic fan will equalize the temperature and keep the house from overheating. It will also get the moisture out of the attic all year long.

In addition, overheating in the attic causes the ceilings of the house to warm up. As a result, more electricity is needed to cool your home. This means wasted energy and higher electricity bills.

Whereas electric fans cost about $10 to $20 a month to run and use about 350 to 400 watts a day, you can run a solar attic fan all day and not have to pay a dime or worry about energy waste.

Lastly, due to air circulation, the temperature of the attic remains lower when running a solar fan. This, in turn, reduces your need for A/C and minimizes heat damage to roof and ceilings. In this vein, solar attic fans are a win win. You save money while also saving the environment.

A solar-powered attic fan requires no wiring and can be simply swapped out for your current passive vent. It reduces attic temperatures by up to 50 degrees and saves you thousands in cooling costs.

$$$ Moderate   🌐🌐🌐

Solar attic ventilation offers a multitude of individual economic and creature-comfort benefits, while at the same time making our world a cleaner and better place to live.

44

Get With the PROGRAM.

Every year, the average household spends upwards of $2,000 a year on energy bills alone – almost half of which is used to heat and cool the home. Eliminate waste, save money, energy, and fight global warming with a programmable thermostat.

With programmable thermostats, the four pre-programmed settings allow you to regulate the temperature of your home at all times – even while you're sleeping or away. As a result, you can be sure that your home is always at the desired temperature – and you don't have to do a thing!

Save around $180 a year!! Programmable thermostats' pre-programmed settings are designed to help you save while maintaining optimal comfort. Adjust them as needed. The important thing is to create a program which reduces the waste created when we neglect to readjust common thermostats as our temperature needs change.

A
ACTION

$2,000
Per year on
energy

$180
Savings with a
programmable
thermostat

$3,600
Over 20 years

**The Green
Millionaire
would have**

$11,340
At the avg. rate
of return
over 20 years

$ $ $ Easy

COOL OFF HEAT   FAN ON   AUTO

Save $3,000 With a Very
BRIGHT IDEA.

70
Light bulbs

$47
Savings per bulb

15x
The lifespan of traditional light bulbs

$3,000
Savings

$1,000
Savings each year

$20,000
Over 20 years

The Green Millionaire would have

$63,000
At the avg. rate of return over 20 years

The average home is using 70 light bulbs. If you changed them out with energy-efficient ones—Compact Fluorescent Light bulbs—you would save over $3,000.

According to a major retailer, each energy-efficient light bulb saves $47 over its lifetime. If every American home replaced just one light bulb with a CFL bulb, we would save enough energy to light more than 3 million homes for a year, save more than $600 million in annual energy costs, and prevent greenhouse gases equivalent to the emissions of more than 800,000 cars. That's just one bulb.

I know these bulbs are a little more expensive up front, but when you consider that CFL bulbs use about 75% less energy than standard incandescent bulbs and last up to 15 times longer, it seems like you will get your money back many times over.

The best places to use CFLs.

The best places to use these lights are in fixtures that are on for periods longer than 20 minutes. Look to use them in areas such as:

Family and living rooms
Kitchen
Dining room
Bedrooms
Outdoors

Choose the bulb that is labeled as equivalent to the incandescent bulb you are replacing. You can find this information right on the product packaging. It will say something like "Soft White 60," or "60 Watt Replacement."

Are CFL's right for you?

Some people say they don't like the light that CFLs give off. True, the early versions did have a more fluorescent feel to them, so that people tended to use them only in garages and attics. But the newer bulbs glow just like regular lightbulbs. There are also CFLs that work on dimmers.

Other people worried that there was too much mercury in CFL bulbs. While there is mercury in them, it is worth noting that the amount is far less than the mercury that is produced in burning coal for electricity.

There really isn't a good excuse anymore for not using these lower-energy bulbs.

Matching the right CFL to the right kind of fixture helps ensure that the bulb will perform.

CFL's are best used in table and floor lamps, outdoor fixtures, sconces, and pendants. This is because open fixtures allow airflow to the bulb.

See how much a you can save by switching to energy-efficient light bulbs using the CFL light-bulb savings calculator.

GE Energy-Smart™ CFL savings calculator.

At www.gelighting.com you can enter the number of regular bulbs you want to replace with Energy-Smart™ CFLs. Click on "calculate" to get your estimated savings.

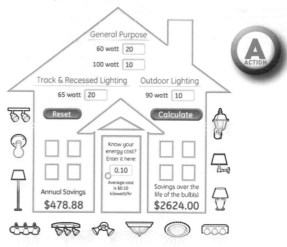

Enter the number of regular bulbs you want to replace with Energy Smart™ CFLs. Click "calculate" to get your estimated savings.

$$ Easy

Have Your Biggest FAN Follow You Around.

Take a portable fan anywhere you go in the house and point it at yourself. This will keep you 10-20 degrees cooler. (We don't suggest taking it in the shower, though.) I do this at home, and even at my gym, which is in an old building that doesn't have air conditioning. I set up a fan to keep me cool while working out. At first people thought it strange, but now they want to use my fan.

Why cool the entire house when you just need to cool your immediate surroundings? The same goes for heating the house. A space heater is a very efficient way of heating just one room.

$ $	**Easy**	

A breeze across our body helps evaporate the small amount of sweat on our skin. This can actually make you feel up to 20 degrees cooler.

How Dangerous Is Your SHOWER?

We're not talking about a psycho waiting to attack you while you shower. So how dangerous can a shower be? It's just steaming hot water, right?

Consider chlorine. We all know it's good for keeping bacteria out of the water. But we also know it's not good for us, and that it's inherent in the water that comes out of the tap. That's why tap water tastes the way it does.

What if you wanted to eliminate chlorine from the water? What's the best way to release it? Answer: Heat it up and turn it into fine mist. And if for some unhealthy reason you wanted to breath it in, then you'd stick your head right into the steam cloud.

Well, that's what a shower is. You absorb more chlorine while showering than you would from drinking 100 glasses of tap water.

I recently changed my shower-head to one that removes the chlorine, and that is also "low flow" for good measure. Now, when I'm in the shower, I drink the water. It tastes like rain.

If you've ever swam in a chlorinated pool, it's likely that you're already aware that chlorine robs hair and skin of moisture. What you probably don't know is that taking a shower without a filter exposes you to far more chlorine than a pool ever could. This is due to the vaporization of chlorine in steam and hot water. Try a shower filter!! You will notice healthier hair and skin straight away.

These filtered shower-heads install in seconds and can make a big difference in the amount of chlorine and other toxic chemicals you breathe in.

While you will save on the amount of water you use in the shower, it is the long-term health benefits that really count.

The 5-Minute Shower.

Impossible!

As Americans we really, really love our shower time. Why else would we spend so much time taking one everyday? Shorter showers just seem unfair and unrealistic, so most of us are inclined to bypass this particular green tip.

But we can't ignore the fact that the average 10-minute shower using a conventional shower-head uses approximately 90 gallons of water.

So what can we do? Install a low-flow shower-head and a water filter—and relax.

Why?

Low-flow shower-heads save 60 percent on your water usage, and using a filter removes residue chemicals from your water so you're not drenching your skin in toxins. Plus, you won't be inhaling chlorine vapors from the steam for 10 minutes a day.

This leads to a healthier shower. And if you can relax while showering and focus on the pleasant experience of hot water pounding down upon you, instead of thinking about the stresses of the day, then your shower will be a much more rejuvenating experience. Also, if you're conscious that you had a hand in the quality of the water coming out of your shower through a filter, you'll be more inclined to shower less in order to prolong the life of the filter.

You breathe in more chlorine in a 5-minute shower than you absorb by drinking 100 glasses of water. A shower-head filter can eliminate almost all of the chlorine. This will improve your health, and your hair and skin.

$ Easy

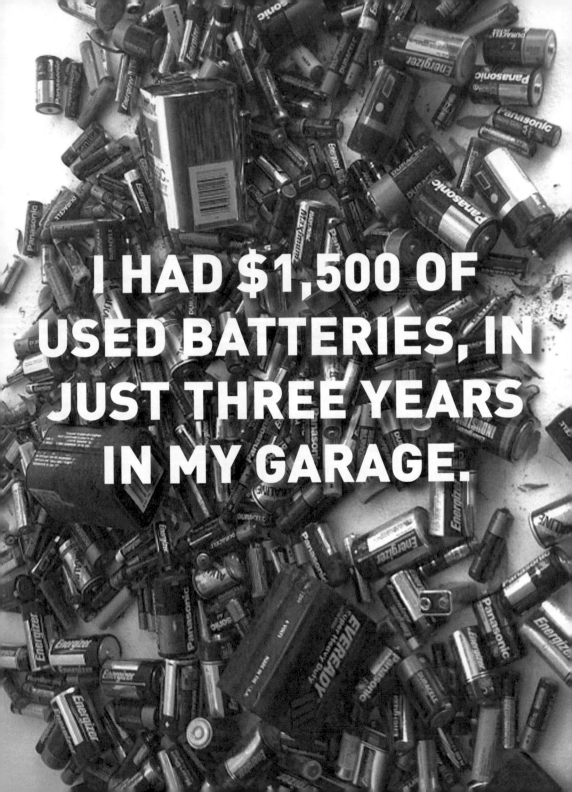

I HAD $1,500 OF USED BATTERIES, IN JUST THREE YEARS IN MY GARAGE.

I try to use hand-cranked flashlights wherever I can. I love them. They always work. I keep them under the sink, in the garage, behind the TV. These new flashlights are amazing, and, if you're like me, who uses a flashlight infrequently, when you do finally get around to using one you usually find the battery is dead and leaking acid.

I especially don't like those big batteries that cost $10, which you never use more than once anyway.

Also, hand-cranked flashlights have bulbs that never break because they are LEDs and last for a long time.

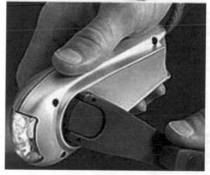

Some of them even have AM/FM radios included that are also hand-cranked. They're perfect for emergencies, and for when you otherwise must know what's going on.

You can even charge your cell phone with them. This is a real life-saver for me when I travel. My phone always dies, and I can seldom find a place to charge it.

Truly an amazing invention.

$ $	Easy	🌐🌐

WHY

can't regular batteries work like cell-phone batteries?

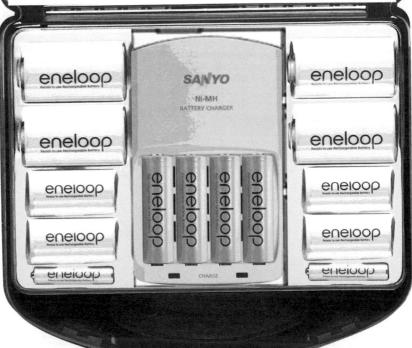

120
Batteries a year

$2
Avg. cost

$240
Savings each year

$4,800
Over 20 years

The Green Millionaire would have

$15,120
At the avg. rate of return over 20 years

Finally, some enterprising companies are saying enough is enough and coming out with new technologies that will allow batteries to work just as well after a thousand charges as they did after the first charge. That was the problem with the first-generation batteries—they just didn't recharge that well after the first few times.

All batteries are basically the same. The only variation is the size.

$$$ Easy

Where do the batteries go?

Recently, I wondered what my family did with our discarded batteries. To my horror, I found a treasure chest containing hundreds and hundreds of batteries in a big tub out in the garage. Well beyond the thousands of wasted dollars that the batteries represented, I became anxious about the effect of so many batteries buried in the earth after being dumped in the landfill. And not just those discarded by our family, but from the hundred-million families that consume the same amount of batteries we do.

Across America, 15,000,000,000 batteries are consumed every year. If you put all those batteries end to end, that's a trip to the moon and back. There are batteries that we all use in our cell phones, video cameras, razors, and tooth brushes that are far more efficient than these old alkaline batteries, which, according to advertising, just keep "going and going." See how marketing makes us think about things? People even compare their own endurance levels to that insidious bunny.

So why aren't regular batteries as efficient as the ones in our cell phones?

They could be, but the battery companies are getting so rich making batteries that last just one charge that there is no incentive for them to change.

The Coolest
Gifts Are GREEN.

One of the best ways to help others become green is to give them green gifts. Start them small. Soon they will see how going green and saving money can set them on their way to becoming a Green Millionaire.

This is a great conversation starter in your favorite coffee shop: a porcelain version of the paper cup. Just imagine how many paper cups this will replace.

You can save up to 10% on your fuel costs by keeping your tires properly inflated. Plus, your tires will last longer, saving you money and the planet less waste.

Go iGreen. Gotta have that iPod? Find out how to have your music without the excess packaging and transportation costs that come with it.

One-third of all waste is food. Add a composting pail to your kitchen for vegetables or coffee grounds. It's amazingly convenient. Then take it outside to freshen up that garden.

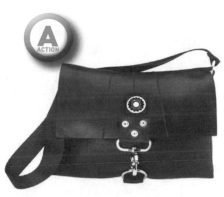

These bags are made from recycled inner-tubes and just look cool. There are also belts and wallets available.

If you are on the go, this solar "juice bag" will keep your iPod and phone charged. It's so easy, and perfect for the student and business traveler. Just add sunlight.

When you're on the run, keep your coffee hot in an insulated cup to avoid those unnecessary trips to the coffee store.

$25 Gift card

Gift cards are great green gifts. Think of how much wrapping paper will be eliminated, to say nothing of return trips to the store.

Inexpensive, reusable bags that you carry to the store not only negate the accumulation of hundreds of disposable bags over the year, but look great too.

Little did we know how healthful our old stainless steal lunch boxes really were. Overexposure to plastic is now known to be toxic to our lunch! Here's the coolest stainless steal lunch box ever, with separate compartments for everything.

How much does it cost to go to WORK?

It is staggering how much it costs just to get to work every day. These are costs we don't even think about. But when it is so difficult to make ends meet these days, it might make sense to cut the commute.

Gas ($4 a gallon x 20mpg)	30 miles a day x 236 days a year	$1,416
Parking	$5 a day	$1,180
25% maintainance	Tires, oil changes, tune-up, etc. ($1,000 yr.)	$250
Tolls	$2 a day	$472
25% of car payment	Based on $200 car payment	$800
Child care	$400 a month	$4,800
Lunch	$8 a day	$1,888
Snacks	$2 a day	$472
Coffee and muffin	$4 a day	$944
Clothes	$100 a month	$1,200
Dry cleaning	$30 a month	$360
TOTAL		**$13,582**
How much you'd have to make before taxes to net $13,582	Assuming 38% is deducted from your paycheck for federal and state taxes, plus FICA, etc.	$21,731

Give yourself a $21,000 raise by not showing up for work.

$13,582
Annual cost to go to work

$271,640
Over 20 years

The Green Millionaire would have

$855,666
At the avg. rate of return over 20 years

$$$$ Moderate   ◉◉◉◉

If you're looking for a way to work from home, you're not alone. Whether you're hoping to bring in a little extra money, contribute to your household finances, or simply be available for your children, thousands of people have found that working from home is their best solution.

One great environmental thing you can do is to work from home. I will show you how to make a compelling argument to your boss to work from home at least one day a week. Imagine the savings from gas to lunches, from clothes to parking, tolls, and more. Now is a great time to help the environment by working from home. Also, I will tell you about some interesting business opportunities that you can take advantage of from home, or anywhere you are.

Eleven great ways to convince your boss that you should work from home:

1. Submit a written proposal.

2. Start with one day a week (not a Friday).

3. Don't stipulate a time period, just propose to see how it works.

4. Start doing projects from home in your own time.

5. Make sure you are known as the reliable person in your office—not one to exploit goodwill.

6. Take this instead of a raise. Most companies are struggling these days and may welcome keeping a good employee with this offer.

7. It could free up resources at the office, such as computers and office space.

8. Explain that you are having difficulty with the expenses of commuting.

9. Explain how good this would be for the environment.

10. Just start doing it and see what happens. (Only if you feel pretty secure in your job.)

11. Talk to your human-resources people about existing programs your company may already have in place.

With computers and Internet access so readily available, this means new, better-paying opportunities for people who want the flexibility and convenience of careers that don't require an office cubicle or a long work commute.

I work from home, from coffee shops, even from the beach, and it has made me realize that I don't need to be in the office eight hours a day. It's more important that I be the one to pick up my kids from school than to stand by the water cooler. Remember, the Green Millionaire doesn't just have money—he or she has a great lifestyle.

Here's a list of jobs you can do in your PAJAMAS.

The Top Home-Based Business Ideas

The thought of starting your own home-based business, or of just working from home, can be overwhelming. There are so many options. However, there are many tried-and-true, home-based businesses that may be just what you're looking for.

Medical claims billing.
This industry is one of the most popular work-from-home businesses; the medical field is certainly healthy these days.

Home tutoring.
You can start a business tutoring students by advertising at schools, the rec center, and other places frequented by families. Maybe start by tutoring some other families at your kid's school.

Consulting.
With the economy in a downturn, companies want to save money by hiring consultants instead of staff. If you are an expert in your industry, such as finance, marketing, or mediation, consider beginning your own consulting business.

Child-care services.
Turn your love for kids into one of the most popular home-based business opportunities. No experience necessary, just patience.

Travel Agent.

Many travel companies use home-based agents to book hotels, cruises, and flights. You can even get a commission on these calls.

Accounting.

A great business to do from home with little client contact and flexible hours. There are many franchises and opportunities available for certified public accountants. Check out the Web site of the American Institute of Certified Public Accountants.

Web design.

If you enjoy being artistic and feel you can design quality Web sites, how about turning your skills into a home-based business? Web designers tend to be well-compensated for their efforts. All that is needed is a computer and the right software.

Desktop publishing.

Like Web design, desktop publishing is an easy work-from-home business. Designing everything from annual reports to menus, this work can be a fantastic way to show your creative side. It can also be very rewarding, and you can get basic training online with some great tutorials.

Remodeling.

If you are a weekend carpenter or handyman around the house, you can turn your skills into your own business. You could find fixer houses to remodel, which right now are especially cheap.

Home inspection.

Maybe you'd rather tell people what they should fix. The National Association of Certified Home Inspectors Web site provides information on becoming certified to inspect homes.

Wedding planner.

If you like putting together parties and planning events, this could be the perfect fit for you. There are numerous certification courses online.

Computer repair.

Does everyone call you when they have a computer problem? Why not start getting paid for fixing hard drives and software? Check out Geeks on Call America and Rescue.com—they have some interesting franchise opportunities.

Cleaning service.

This wouldn't be my first choice but some people love to clean. One way to go is with a franchise. JaniKing is one of the largest franchisers in the cleaning market.

Carpet-cleaning service.

There are many popular franchises such as ServiceMaster Clean and Cleanpro that allow you to start your own carpet-cleaning business and receive the equipment and training. Clean up in the carpet-cleaning business!

Transcription services.

You can easily work from home for a variety of different companies, especially in the medical and legal fields. It might be good to take a speed typing course since you will be paid by the word.

A ACTION

www.workathomecareers.com
WorkAtHomeCareers.com provides pre-screened work at home jobs, articles, videos, and scam avoidance information.
www.hbwm.com
Home-Based Working Moms™ is a professional association and online community of parents who work at home, and for those who would like to.

$ $ $ $ Involved

The iPOD of Books.

I was lukewarm about this technology. I thought the screen would be difficult to read and I would get tired looking it.

That was until I tried one. The on-screen image looks like it is printed on the surface of the screen. I'm not sure how they do that. The screen actually looks like it's printed, and you can't help but touch it to see if it has a papery feel.

People I know are addicted to this gadget. Last year you had to pay double its price on Ebay just to get one.

It can hold up to 200 books and you can have your daily newspaper delivered to it, as well as magazines.

It's a wireless device, so you don't even need to plug it in to get the Sunday paper or the latest Grisham novel.

It is lighter than a typical paperback.

The books you download cost about half the price of the paper versions, and magazines are about $1.50 a month. Incredible.

But imagine how many trees this would save, not to mention all the transportation and delivery costs of daily newspapers.

Thirty million trees are cut down to produce books in the U.S. annually.

Sales of these ebooks have been rising 50% a year—not bad for a country in recession. Maybe there are more Green Millionaires out there than we thought.

Sidebar

25
Books per year

365
Newspapers

3
Magazine subscriptions

$765
Spent on reading materials

$389
Savings

$7,780
Savings over 20 years

The Green Millionaire would have

$24,507
At the avg. rate of return over 20 years

Worldwide, 453 million trees are cut down for newspapers annually.

What a shame to cut down these pristine forests when it is so needless. Technologies are available to avoid this.

$$$ Easy ⊕⊕⊕⊕

It weighs less than a paperback and can hold 200 books, magazines and newspapers.

68

The Scariest Vampire is On When the TV Is OFF.

It's called "vampire energy." It literally sucks the energy from appliances while they're "asleep." Vampire energy costs the U.S. $3 billion a year.

$140
Avg. monthly electric bill

$1,680
Avg. yearly electric bill

$168
Annual savings

$3,600
Over 20 years

The Green Millionaire would have

$10,584
At the avg. rate of return over 20 years

Anything that has a standby mode is drawing power, even when you're not using it. Plasma TVs, DVD players, electric toothbrushes, cell phone chargers, fax machines, shredders, lamps, fans, modems, routers, speakers, scanners, and CD players—all stay on when you're not around. It's like you're letting gremlins live in your house rent-free.

As an example, a plasma TV can consume $162 a year when it is in the standby mode. That mode exists just so the TV will come on instantly when you hit the remote. Are those few seconds you save worth hundreds of dollars a year?

A simple device can turn these things off and save you a lot of money over the course of a few years.

The biggest turn-off.

This device also comes with a remote control that turns off all the devices you want in one fell swoop.

How much energy is wasted by leaving an appliance on when you're not using it? This simple device can go right on the wall (which saves bending down to switch off all those buttons), and turns off up to eight devices, while leaving two permanently on.

There are other kinds, too, that work by motion sensors, or can tell when you're not using a certain appliance.

You need a powerstrip and surge protector anyway, so why not get one that will pay for itself? It turns off all of the appliances except the ones you want kept on. Plus, it has a remote so you don't have to crawl around behind the TV.

$$$ Easy   ◑◑

The California Energy Commission estimates standby power losses in the average household to be as much as 15% of household electricity use.

They say knowledge is
POWER.

Actually, we believe with this device that knowledge is saving power. The "Kill A Watt" is a simple device that plugs into a socket. You then plug in whatever other electrical device you want. Leave it on for a while and you'll see how much each appliance is costing you over time. You'll discover that it may save you money to switch to a gas-powered clothes dryer, or get a more energy-efficient refrigerator. You'll also see the vampire energy being drawn from the wall, and how the appliances you don't even think about as being power hogs are actually costing you a lot of money every year.

Now you can cut your energy costs and find out which appliances are actually worth keeping plugged in. You'll know for certain if it is time for a new refrigerator, or if that old air conditioner is still saving you money. With this device you'll know "watts" killing you. (Sorry.)

$$$ Easy   🌍🌍

Here are some typical power usages of common household appliances, as measured in watts.

Dishwasher - 1200-1500
Desktop computer - 80-150
Garbage disposal - 450
Computer printer - 100
Washing machine - 500
9" disc sander - 1200
TV (25" color) - 150
Coffee pot - 200
Garage door opener - 350
Coffee-maker - 800
Ceiling fan - 10-50
Toaster - 800-1500
Table fan - 10-25
Electric blanket - 200
Blender - 300
Blow-dryer - 1000
Microwave - 600-1500
Shaver - 15
Waffle iron - 1200
Hedge trimmer - 450
Hot plate - 1200
Weed eater - 500
Frying pan - 1200
Laptop computer - 20-50
1/4" drill - 250
3" belt sander - 1000
TV (19" color) - 70
12" chain saw - 1100
14" band saw - 1100
Upright vacuum - 200-700
VCR - 40
Handheld vacuum - 100
CD player - 35
Sewing machine - 100
Portable stereo - 10-30
Refrigerator, 20 cubic feet - 540
Iron - 1000
Clock radio - 1
Electric clothes dryer - 4000
Satellite dish - 30
Electric clock - 3
Fan heater 150-1000
Furnace blower - 300-1000
Room A/C - 1000
Central A/C - 2000-5000
Electric mower - 1500

If we could increase gas mileage
by just 1 MPG...

...it would be like discovering a whole new
oil reserve producing **650,000**
barrels of oil a day.

The TRUE Cost of Owning a Car.

1
Avg. sedan

$20,600
Purchase price

$8,600
Costs per year

$172,000
Over 20 years

The Green Millionaire would have

$541,800
At the avg. rate of return over 20 years

The true cost of owning a car is huge. It is 20% of your annual income.

The average family works two full months each year to pay for every vehicle they own. If you could have just one car in the family then you would reach your Green Millionaire status with just this savings tip alone. But whether you drive one car or two, you will save real money here.

Remember: Just because the purchase price of a car might be low, this doesn't make it any cheaper to drive.

The purchase price is only the beginning.

You have to wonder if the new car smell is worth over $500K over the next 20 years.

Here are the other costs involved with owning a car:

Depreciation:
A new car can lose 50% or more of its value in five years. It loses 20% just driving off the lot.

Financing:
The interest rate payments can amount to as much as 50% of the price of the car over its lifetime.

Insurance:
Insurance rates keep going through the roof. And the cheap rates usually don't cover essential things.

Taxes:
Up to 8% of the purchase price goes to Uncle Sam.

Registration:
You likely pay hundreds of dollars to register your car every year.

Fuel:
The average car logs 15,000 miles per year, while average fuel economy is about 20 mpg (which is actually worse than it was in the 1970s when

The true cost of owning a $21,000 vehicle over 5 years

	Year 1	Year 2	Year 3	Year 4	Year 5	5 Year
Depreciation	$2,815	$2,635	$2,320	$2,057	$1,846	$11,673
Financing	$1,486	$1,206	$901	$569	$208	$4,370
Insurance	$1,802	$1,865	$1,930	$1,998	$2,028	$9,623
Taxes & Fees	$1,883	$153	$136	$121	$107	$2,400
Fuel	$2,029	$2,090	$2,153	$2,218	$2,285	$10,775
Maintenance	$228	$523	$337	$941	$1,839	$3,868
Repairs	$0	$125	$298	$298	$435	$858
Yearly Totals	$10,243	$8,472	$7,902	$8,202	$8,748	$43,567

fuel economy was 22 mpg). So with gas recently around $4 a gallon, you're paying around $3,000 a year.

Maintenance:

Brakes, tires, oil changes, wiper blades, etc. These costs can be unexpected and add up to hundreds of dollars per year.

Repairs:

Transmissions, windshields, fuel pumps, suspensions. You never know what will fail on a car and drastically affect your budget that month.

So let's say you buy a $21,000 car. How much will it cost you to own it over five years?

Some people can afford to buy a car but they can't afford to own it. Understanding a vehicle's TCO (Total Cost to Own) is extremely important to a person on a fixed budget. Any way you look at it, it's expensive to own a car, especially when you also consider that you'd have to make around $60,000 before taxes over five years to purchase an ordinary new vehicle. And remember, that car is only worth $14,000 after 5 years.

As you can see, owning an average car can cost you $43,567 over five years. A Prius is $40,618. A Mercedes costs $69,197. Even a three-year-old car costs $38,118 to own over five years.

$$$$ Moderate   ⊙⊙⊙⊙

If you are like the average car owner, you will work for two months to pay for your vehicle. That's two months out of every year.

Average Annual Household Expenditures, 2004	
Item	Proportion of Total Expenditure
shelter (home mortgage or rent)	32%
car ownership & operating expenses	17%
food	13%
pensions & Social Security contributions	10%
utilities	7%
health care	6%
entertainment	5%
clothing	4%
household furnishing	4%
education	2%

source: BLS Current Expenditure Shares Table
U.S. Department of Labor Bureau of Labor Statistics
http://www.bls.gov/cex/

LOVE
The One You're With.

The most energy-efficient car you can own is the one you already have, no matter what kind of gas guzzler it is. I know that sounds crazy (you probably thought I would be advising you to buy a Prius), but consider this: If you take existing materials from an engine, rebore the cylinders a little wider, ad new pistons, and replace all the seals, you have an engine rebuilt to a higher specification than the original, and one that costs merely a fraction of a brand new engine.

Some cars even appreciate in value over time.

The amount of energy that goes into making a car, no matter how fuel-efficient, is far greater than the cost of driving the vehicle 200,000 miles. All the sheet metal, seats, and wiring have to be manufactured and transported here for assembly. If you really want to treat yourself, get a can of that new car smell, buy a great stereo and maybe a navigation system, and relish the thought that not buying a new car has saved you thousands in depreciation and saved the planet untold in squandered resources. The fact is, cars are just as inefficient today as they were 100 years ago.

$ $ $ Easy

How about saving thousands if you drive a classic? Some of these older cars aren't that bad on gas mileage—just make sure the engine is up to today's cleaner-air standards.

How To ENJOY Your Commute.

Interestingly, if you look at some of the richest areas in the U.S., you'll find that the people who live there take the bus, the ferry, and train. These are great ways to get work done, catch up on a book, or watch your video iPod.

I live in Los Angeles. A few years ago, my kids asked me what the numbers on the front of a bus were for. They had no concept of bus routes. When I was young living in London, a bus was how you got around; it couldn't have been easier.

If you look at the major cities in the world, they all share one thing in common that allows them to be so livable and (relatively) uncongested by traffic: fantastic mass transit systems. Los Angeles has one of the most beautiful train systems in the country; people ride the train just to see the various artworks in each of the stations. But still, not enough people take the train. (Wait till it extends to the beach!)

In the days before we were all green, we rode public transport just to save money. We didn't know we were being green.

Years ago I rode the ferry to work in San Francisco. I remember one guy who would go outside in the wind and his comb-over would come unraveled, which would always make me laugh.

Taking mass transit can also be more relaxing than sitting in traffic. You get to meet some interesting people. On the ferry there were a number of people who met and got married. On Fridays there was a jazz band. Authorities wanted to put a faster boat into service but the passengers objected; they wanted the longer commute.

Parking in the larger cities is crazy. In New York you can pay $40 a day and more, and San Francisco is not far behind, with $30 parking. Miami is $20.

Toll roads can add up.

It is these expenses, which you pay every day, that really bleed you over the years.

I used to ride my bike everywhere. I loved it. It gave me time to think. Plus, I didn't need to go to the gym to ride a stationary version.

$$$ Easy   ☺☺☺

Every day I used to take the ferry to San Francisco. There were no two days when the ride felt the same. I took my bike and loved every minute of it.

Transportation

RIDE-SHARE
With a New Friend, Maybe Your Boss.

40	Mile commute
$8	Gas
$5	Parking
$3,380	Cost of getting to work a year. Not including cost of owning a car.
4	People in carpool
75%	Reduction of costs
$50,700	Savings

The Green Millionaire would have

$159,705
At the avg. rate of return over 20 years

If you want to drive somewhere, find out if someone else is going your way. Let's say you want to go skiing in Park City, Utah, and you live in Phoenix, Arizona. Maybe someone else is going and you can share costs. Or what if you have a regular commute of 50 miles from San Jose to San Francisco—maybe there is someone else who has that same route and timetable. Let's start sharing our resources. If every car on the road was occupied with four passengers there would be 75% less traffic.

My measure of how much I like someone is proportionate to how far I would want to travel in a car with that person. Some people I could only go around the block with; others I could drive cross-country. The point is, find someone you like chatting with and start carpooling. The Internet has made it very easy to find people who match your needs.

You can check out alternetrides.com and rideshare.com. Also, craigslist.org is a great resource.

I have found that driving and chatting with someone makes any trip seem a lot shorter. I used to drive 100 miles roundtrip each day with a colleague. We would talk about a variety of things, mostly office gossip. But I still remember those conversations, and I made a friend for life.

You must know a few people at work who live near you and who smell nice. You can split the costs and get to know each other a little better. You never know, it might even be your boss.

$$$	Easy	☺☺☺

Never Pay For Gas Again, REALLY.

Drive a frybrid, not a hybrid.

What if you didn't want to pay for gas at all anymore? I am going to show you right here how you can avoid ever having to pay for gas again. Gas is made from a hydrocarbon that is very similar to another kind of oil—vegetable oil. Gallons and gallons of this stuff are thrown away by restaurants every day from their deep fryers. They pay someone to take it away. Go to greenmillionaire.com and I'll show you how you can drive for free using this oil. And all it takes is 20 minutes to modify your engine. Many Mercedes, Jeeps, and Volkswagens are driving around using vegetable oil right now. They don't call them hybrids, they call them frybrids.

Not only is the gas free, but you can get up to 69 mpg (VW Jetta), or 30-40 mpg (2009 Ford F-150).

A good friend of mine and his family are driving using this oil. We used to find it funny and now they're the ones laughing. Their gas station is the local sushi restaurant. They save $7,500 a year on gas. And I can show you how. Plus, you can always use regular gas if you need to.

Make $500 an hour and never have to pay for gas again.

The Green Millionaire is resourceful. Especially at $80 a tank. It is possible to make $500 an hour by collecting just two 55-gallon containers. You could sell oil to your friends.

Biodiesel is stored in 55-gallon drums outside restaurants. They are ecstatic when someone comes and takes it away so they don't have to pay a renderer to do it. You are doing them a favor, and vice-versa.

That oil drum has $250 of vegetable oil in it. Not a bad price.

If you had taken the money you'd saved and bought Apple stock 10 years ago, you'd have six times that money now.

Veggie cars and trucks get the same gas mileage as their diesel counterparts, and if you're unable to find an accommodating restaurant, you can always fill up on regular diesel.

These engines are just as clean as their catalytic- converting counterparts.

15,000
Miles a year

$4
A gallon

20
Avg. mpg

$3,000
Cost of gas a year

$60,800
Savings over 20 years

The Green Millionaire would have

$189,000
At the avg. rate of return over 20 years

This VW Golf TDI gets 69 mpg and can run on free WVO (waste vegetable oil) with a conversion kit.

$ $ $ $ Moderate   🌍🌍🌍

2008:Exxon Mobil had a
bigger profit
than any company in history.

$ $ $ Easy

| 15,000 |
| Miles a year |

| $4 |
| A gallon |

| 20 |
| Avg. mpg |

| $3,000 |
| Cost of gas a year |

| $60,800 |
| Savings over 20 years |

The Green Millionaire would have

| $189,000 |
| At the avg. rate of return over 20 years |

The high gas prices of 2008 left consumers furious. Now the number-one thing people look for in a vehicle is fuel economy. Not styling, not performance. Fuel economy. That's a huge change.

UNLEADED

ARM

UNLEADED PLUS

LEG⁹

Fuel Additives.

If they conserve fuel and increase performance, why don't the gas companies just put them in the gas?

Duh!

Would you take a pay cut if you didn't have to? No, and neither would they. While fuel additives can dramatically affect the performance of your car's engine and reduce emissions, oil companies have nothing to gain from improving your engine's performance, so they do nothing. They have been happy to produce the same product for the last 100 years, while doing very little to improve efficiency.

As part of writing this book, I wanted to see if there was a simple way of reducing our consumption of gas. I looked at many different options and was disappointed—I thought if someone actually could save you gas they would be able to document it.

So I was about to give up when I discovered a company that had patented a formula that was first noted 60 years ago to help save our oil reserves.

This company had created a fuel reformulator, not an additive.

When the scientist who discovered it presented it to the oil company he worked for, he was put out to pasture. The company didn't feel it was good for business to sell less gas. So the idea lay dormant for over three decades.

The inventor spent the next 33 years trying to get his invention in front of the public. He had some success with industrial applications and within the military, but it is only recently that his invention has become widely available to the public. In fact, the U.S. Marine Corps tested the product and recorded an average fuel economy increase of 35%.

This additive is not petroleum-based; it is mineral-based. It coats the cylinders of the engine, creating a tight seal, which means no leaks around the pistons. It also basically polishes the surface of the cylinders, reducing friction, which causes engine heat and therefore improves gas mileage. It also increases the octane from 89 to 90 and higher, which means better performance in your engine. You could switch to a grade lower of octane if you use this additive, and save money that way.

The owner of the company showed me a 1929 Rolls Royce he owned. The car had never passed a smog test until he put this product in the gas tank.

The green benefit from this technology isn't just better gas mileage, but emission reduction up to an unbelievable 89%, which is documented by major government bodies.

I am glad to find that these entrepreneurs stuck with this product, as it could have a significant effect on our oil consumption and therefore the health of the planet.

Fuel reformulators can drastically reduce emissions around 80%, and gas mileage by up to 20%, or $600 per vehicle per year.

Inflation Is GOOD For the Planet.

2
Vehicles

10
PSI under-inflated

5%
Extra gas a year

25%
Reduction of tire lifespan

$300
Gas savings

$200
Savings on tires

$1,000
Savings over 20 years

The Green Millionaire would have

$3,150
At the avg. rate of return over 20 years

If you're like me, you probably only check your tires when they look a little flat. I recently found I'd been driving around on about 10 psi on two of my tires. One of the 2008 U.S. presidential candidates made fun of tire inflation as a petty way to combat global warming.

So I decided to find out if it was fact or fiction.

The EPA states that for every 2 psi of pressure under the recommended level you suffer a 1% loss of gas mileage. If, like me, your car is 10 psi under-inflated, you may not even notice it by visual inspection, but under-inflation could add an extra 5% to your vehicle expenses each year, or around $300 for two cars.

The problem is that it's difficult to find a gas station anymore that has an air pump, let alone one that has an accurate pressure gauge. Plus, they now charge 75 cents or more for the privilege of checking your own tires (aren't they making enough on the gas?).

Why not get your own electric pump? These new machines can inflate your tires in seconds. And they're far more accurate than the ones at the gas station.

Another benefit to inflating your tires properly is that they will last longer. Under-inflation is a major cause of tire wear, so if you can increase the life of your tires 25% you can save another $200 a year for two cars.

If everyone in the U.S. were to properly inflate their tires, it could reduce our collective need for oil by over 650,000 barrels a day. That would be like discovering a massive new reserve, or saving 13 billion gallons of gas a year.

Most importantly, it would save 271 billion pounds of carbon dioxide being released into the atmosphere.

Seems like a huge savings for sacrificing just a few seconds every month.

$ $ $ Easy   🌐🌐🌐

One gallon of gas gives off about 20 lbs. of CO2. How is this possible if gas only weighs 6 lbs. a gallon? Easy. The carbon in the gasoline combines with the oxygen in the air to form carbon dioxide. So the CO2 comes from the reaction of the gas and the air.

If everyone properly inflated their tires it would save 13 billion gallons of gas a year.

Uncle Sam WANTS YOU
To Have Billions To Go Green.

The Green Millionaire knows how to use other people's money to achieve his or her goals.

If any of you owns your own business, you're well aware of how much the government favors business people. There are billion-dollar programs in place to save your business money and make you a Green Millionaire even faster.

This is thinking like a Green Millionaire: What's good for the environment is also great for business.

Even if you don't own your house or apartment, you can still get help from Uncle Sam.

Why use your own money to become a GREEN MILLIONAIRE?

The federal government, as well as every state, city, and utility company, has money it wants to give you. It's just not very good at getting the word out. Much of the money goes unclaimed because people don't know it's available. It's almost as if the government feels like it should offer these programs but doesn't want you to know about them.

There are literally billions of dollars out there in the form of grants, tax credits, and really low-interest loans to help you achieve your goal of being a Green Millionaire.

All millionaires know one thing: OPM = other people's money. Here are a couple examples of how to leverage OPM to achieve your own goals:

One city is helping you lower your energy bills by paying you to install solar panels. We're talking about giving away $10,000 or more to individuals who want to reduce their energy costs.

In many parts of the country, cities will pay for weather-stripping, CFL light bulbs, a new refrigerator, insulation, water-heater jackets, and pipe insulation. They will not only pay for the materials but they will come out and install. This represents thousands of dollars of work that you don't have to pay for. You just need to know where to look.

California allocates $3 billion of state funds to help people go green.

Los Angeles allocates over $300 million to upgrade the energy-efficiency of your house, for FREE, while also helping to pay for new appliances.

A ACTION

You can get a solar energy system for free in six states, and for under $1,200 in 20 states.

Massachusetts has $68 million in grants for businesses to install solar panels, up to $1.6 million per business. Homeowners can earn close to $2,000 in state-sponsored rebates for weatherizing, or installing energy-efficient appliances, such as a new furnace or thermostat.

New York will give building owners up to $2 million in tax breaks per building by going green. And the same goes for renters.

SOME QUICK WAYS TO CONSERVE ENGERY IN YOUR HOME.

1. Reverse indoor ceiling fans for summer and winter use.

2. When using central air conditioning, leave vents open in unused rooms.

3. Do not raise the thermostat on your water heater higher than 120°.

4. Set thermostat for 68° in winter and 78° in summer.

5. Turn down or shut off your water heater when away from home for an extended time.

6. Turn lights off even when leaving a room for a short time.

7. Install energy-efficient windows.

8. Minimize door-opening when using the oven, which reduces oven temperature by 25° to 30°.

9. Use your dryer more effiently by cleaning the lint filter after every load.

10. Unplug appliances you rarely use.

11. Whenever possible, use a microwave oven instead of a conventional oven or stove.

12. Use electric appliances only when you need them.

13. Replace or clean air filters on your air conditioning unit once a month.

14. Turn off lights, computers, or any appliance not in use.

15. Only purchase appliances with the "Energy Star" label, which use less electricity than nonsuch models.

16. Avoid washing clothes in hot water.

17. Save money and energy by using compact fluorescent light bulbs.

18. Keep your water heater wrapped in an insulated blanket.

19. When away from home in summer, set your thermostat higher; in winter, lower.

20. Insulate your home.

21. Install weather-stripping around doors and windows.

22. At work, turn off electrical equipment when going home.

23. Take advantage of natural cooling techniques: plant trees to shade your home.

24. Likewise for outside air-conditioning units.

25. Set your refrigerator no higher than 38°, and your freezer no higher than 5°.

26. Use cold water whenever possible.

27. Sync your outdoor lights to a timer.

28. Buy electricity produced by low- or zero-pollution utilities.

29. Save $200 a year by closing your chimney flue when not using the fireplace.

SOME QUICK WAYS TO REDUCE TOXICITY IN YOUR HOME.

The cost of treating the harmful effects of toxic chemicals could severely affect your financial future, not to mention your health. A report came out in California recently that the toxic chemicals we come in contact with on a daily basis cost the state $28 billion a year.

1. Have the paint in your home tested for lead. If lead is present, cover the paint with wall paper or other material. Do not sand or burn it off.

2. Seek alternatives to household cleaning items that use hazardous chemicals. Consider solutions like baking soda, scouring pads, or plain water.

3. Buy only as much paint as you need.

4. If you must use a toxic substance, use the least amount required for an effective, sanitary result.

5. Eliminate use of items containing mercury, and properly dispose of all preexisting items containing mercury.

6. Avoid using poison and insect killers to eliminate pests. Use traps instead.

7. Test your home for radon.

8. Cedar chips and aromatic herbs are just as effective as mothballs.

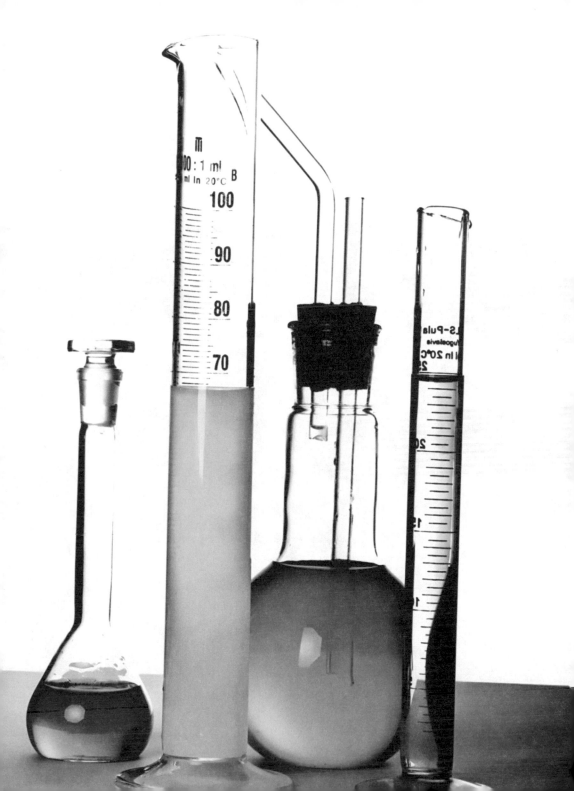

HAVE A GREENER BACK YARD

It's a sad story, but we lost a dog a couple of years ago. He was just sitting in the grass enjoying the sun. We didn't know that the lawn had just been fertilized, and he died two days later from a huge amount of potassium in his blood.

1. If a rake is too low-tech for you, use an electric leaf-blower rather than a gas-powered one.

2. Same goes for your lawn mower.

3. And be sure to leave those grass clippings in the yard—they decompose and return vital nutrients to the soil.

4. Save money and the environment—rent or borrow tools used infrequently, like ladders, chain saws, or party decorations.

5. Don't over-fertilize your yard.

6. Keep use of pesticides to a minimum.

7. Cultivate a wildlife habitat in your own back yard.

8. Water your lawn early in the morning.

9. To control weeds, retain moisture and prevent erosion, use recycled wood chips as mulch.

10. Don't burn leaves or throw them away—put them in a compost heap. Haul debris too large for your composter to a recycler.

11. Outdoor lighting is expensive and the wiring often complex; convert to solar-powered outdoor lights.

WHAT CAN YOU DO AT WORK?

Offices are one of the biggest producers of waste in the U.S. If you could eliminate waste, and therefore costs, you could help your company during these difficult times.

1. Use both sides of the paper when copying or printing.

2. Reuse office supplies like envelopes, folders, and paper clips.

3. Avoid using new envelopes for interoffice mail—send re-usable mailer sheets instead.

4. Save paper by posting memos to a community bulletin board instead of sending a copy to each employee.

5. Correspond by e-mail whenever possible.

6. Use recycled paper.

7. Use discarded paper for scrap paper.

8. Encourage your organization to print documents using soy-based ink, which is less toxic than regular ink.

9. Bring your own coffee mug to work instead of drinking from disposable cups.

HOW TO BREATHE A LITTLE EASIER

Ways To Protect Our Air

1. Encourage your employer to promote flex time or telecommuting.

2. Recycle printer cartridges.

3. Turn off electrical equipment when you leave the office.

4. Report smoking vehicles to your air quality management agency.

5. When air quality is poor, don't burn wood fuel in your wood stove or fireplace.

6. Be alert to slow-burning, smoldering fires, which produce the greatest amount of pollution.

7. Reduce driving by walking or riding your bike whenever possible.

8. Heat your home and water supply using solar power.

9. Use only low-VOC (volatile oganic compound) or water-based paints, stains, finishes, and paint strippers.

10. Use radial tires on your vehicle and keep them properly inflated.

11. Avoid using spray paints in order to minimize harmful emissions.

12. Ignite charcoal barbecues with an electric probe or other alternative to lighter fluid.

13. Wood stoves sold after 1990 are required to meet federal emissions standards, and are more efficient and cleaner-burning.

14. Seasoned wood burns cleaner than green wood.

Water is LIFE.

"You ain't gonna miss your water until your well runs dry."

-Bob Marley

Ways to Use Less Water

1. Fix water leaks.

2. Install water-saving devices on faucets and toilets.

3. Don't run tap continuously while washing dishes.

4. Load dishwasher and washing machine fully before operating.

5. Follow local water-use guidelines.

6. Install a low-flow shower-head.

7. Replace old toilets with newer, more efficient models.

8. Prevent leaks by turning off water supply to washing machine.

Ways to Protect Our Water

1. Disturbed soil absorbs water; revegetate or mulch affected areas as soon as possible.

2. No dumping in storm drains!

3. Pump and inspect your septic tank system regularly.

4. Check your car for leaking fluids, and always recycle motor oil.

5. Don't wash your car in the driveway; take it to the car wash.

6. Learn about your watershed.

Create Less TRASH

1. Extend the life of durable goods through proper care and maintenance.

2. One-third of what we discard is product packaging; seek products packaged efficiently and that minimize waste.

3. Buy reusable products.

4. Buy items in bulk to reduce wasteful packaging.

5. Use consumer reports to locate dependable products that are easily repaired or break-down infrequently.

6. Reuse bags and containers.

7. Use cloth napkins instead of paper.

8. Use biodegradable plates and utensils instead of disposable ones.

9. Use reusable containers to store food instead of aluminum foil and plastic wrap.

10. Shop with a reusable canvas bag instead of using paper or plastic bags.

11. Install rechargeable batteries in commonly used devices.

12. Don't waste old packaging material; reuse cartons and shipping boxes.

13. Compost vegetable scraps.

14. Buy used furniture—it's much cheaper than buying new, and there is a surplus of it.

15. Become familiar with sites like freecycle.org, craigslist.org, and ebay.com.

THE U.S. CREATES 40%
OF GLOBAL WASTE

Less Really Is MORE.

I hope that you have seen there are better ways to consume that require neither radical austerity or deprivation. It has been my intention merely to help us consider alternative choices that do less harm to the planet and to our wallets.

Does it really matter whether you drink water from a plastic bottle or a re-usable one?

Can you tell the difference between electricity generated from solar panels or from coal?

Would working from home be better for your family, your company, and the planet?

Remember, going green isn't an overnight process and you shouldn't be hard on yourself if you aren't perfect right away.

But I hope that you will start seeing the benefits in the short term, and that you will achieve your long-term financial dreams of becoming a Green Millionaire.

Turn Green Savings into Real

WEALTH

A STEP-BY-STEP GUIDE to becoming wealthy even
if you don't think you have any spare money.

NIGEL J. WILLIAMS

Turning Your Green Savings
Into Millions

Saving money is one of those tasks easier said than done. There's more to it than simply spending less money (although that part alone can be challenging). Crucial questions arise, like where will you cut back? How much money will you save? Where will you put it? And how can you make sure it stays there?

What I will introduce you to are methods to help you set realistic goals, keep your spending in check, and, above all, learn how to pay yourself first.

The Green Millionaire savings program does not reward you with a lump sum of cash. It is not like winning the lottery. The money you make you will accumulate little by little, much the same way it trickled out (until that fateful day when you looked up and wondered where all your money went). Imagine, for example, that you have begun to save money by making your own coffee, whether at home or at work, with your own coffee machine. Or that perhaps you stopped drinking soda, or got a soda fountain for the home. Or stopped drinking that crazy bottled water and started using filtered water and a reusable carrier.

In just two months you would have saved:

Coffee	60 days x $3.50 = $210
Soda	60 days x $1.50 = $90
Bottled Water	60 days x $1.50 = $90

 TOTAL for 60 days = $390

My parents used to say, "A dollar saved is a dollar earned," and I've now happily realized that they were wrong. A dollar saved is $1.67 earned because you have to make $1.67 nowadays in order to save a dollar. To know what I'm talking about just look at your paycheck, and note all the money that's skimmed off to pay federal tax, FICA, state taxes, and the rest.

So the $390 you saved in green money is really $651 in earned money. Think about that: You have to earn $651 every 60 days just to cover that daily habit of drinking one soda, one fancy coffee, and one (wasteful) bottled water each day. And if you're like me, those numbers are low. Also, think about how many hours you've had to work to make that money. Or about what else you might have bought with it over the long term, like a fuel-efficient car or a better house. And remember, this is just one small category of savings—there are plenty more out there for you to discover.

Okay, you say, this brings my attention to the money I shouldn't be spending. But how can I actually *realize* that money?

Easy. Decide where you're going to stop spending.

Make a list of all the things in this book (and things you can think of, too) that you feel will not only benefit you personally but help the planet as well. Modifying your behavior will help you start realizing the savings.

FIRST, you need to know how much you've got.

I apologize for doing this to you, but in order to become a Green Millionaire this really is something we all must do: Discover how much money we have to work with in the first place.

Using the chart below, write down all sources of your income. Do it in the way you find easiest, whether by weekly, monthly, or annual amounts.

The goal is to discover what your family's "profit margin" is, and, with luck, this figure will turn out to be a positive number. But even if it isn't we can still get it there.

Now go to it, and I hope you are pleasantly surprised with the results.

WHAT COMES IN

	Weekly	Monthly	Annually
INCOME:			
Wages and Bonuses			
Interest Income			
Investment Income			
Miscellaneous Income			
Income Subtotal			
INCOME TAXES WITHHELD:			
Federal Income Tax			
State and Local Income Tax			
Social Security/Medicare Tax			
Income Taxes Subtotal			
Spendable Income			
TOTAL			

Next, fill in the columns specifying your recurring expenses. Use the far column to note areas where you might be able to cut back in your spending. Areas shaded in green denote "Green Areas of Flexibility," i.e., areas where cutting back will benefit both the environment and your bottom line.

	Weekly	Monthly	Annually	Flexibility? Y/N
HOME:				
Mortgage or Rent				
Homeowners/Renter's Insurance				
Property Taxes				
Home Repairs/Maintenance/HOA Dues				
Home Improvements				
UTILITIES:				
Electricity				
Water and Sewer				
Natural Gas or Oil				
Telephone (land line, cell)				
FOOD:				
Groceries				
Eating Out, Lunches, Snacks				
FAMILY OBLIGATIONS:				
Child Support				
Alimony				
Day Care, Babysitting				
HEALTH AND MEDICAL:				
Insurance (medical, dental, vision)				
Unreimbursed Medical Expenses, Copays				
Fitness (yoga, massage, gym)				
TRANSPORTATION:				
Car Payments				
Gasoline/Oil				
Auto Repairs/Maintenance/Fees				
Auto Insurance				
Other Transportation (tolls, bus, subway, taxis)				
DEBT PAYMENTS:				
Credit Cards				
Student Loans				
Other Loans				
ENTERTAINMENT/RECREATION:				
Cable TV/Videos/Movies				
Computer Expense				
Hobbies				
Subscriptions				
Vacations				
TOTAL				

The green bars indicate the potential "green savings" areas.

Category	How Much You Spend Weekly	How Much You Spend Monthly	How Much You Spend Yearly	Am I Willing To Adopt An Alternative In Order To Cut Expenses? Y/N
EXAMPLE: Driving yourself to work	$100	$400	$4,800	Yes
AUTOMOBILE EXPENSES:				
Gas				
Insurance				
Maintenance				
Car payments				
Repairs				
Registration				
BEVERAGES:				
Coffees, cappuccino, lattes, etc.				
Bottled water				
Soda (vending machines, cans, bottles)				
GOING TO WORK:				
Parking				
Tolls				
Snacks				
Gas				
Dry cleaning				
Clothes				
Coffee on the way				
25% cost of car				
Childcare				
HOME ENERGY:				
Electricity				
Natural gas				
Water				
Sewer				
READING MATERIALS:				
Books				
Magazines				
Newspapers				

Alternative	What Would It Cost To Change?	How Much Would You Save A Year?	What Would The Planet Save?
EXAMPLE: Carpooling	$400/year	$4,400	15,000 lbs. of CO2
AUTOMOBILE EXPENSES:			
Eliminate second or third car			
Consider a more fuel-efficient car			
Get a motorcycle			
Use fuel reformulator; voluntarily reduce gas consumption and emissions			
Convert diesel engine to run on waste vegetable oil for free			
Purchase older, classic vehicle			
BEVERAGES:			
Coffees, cappuccinos, lattes, etc.: Use cappuccino or coffee maker			
Bottled water: Use filtered water and a reusable container			
Soda (vending machines, cans, bottles): Use home soda maker			
GETTING TO WORK:			
Start a home-based business (the average makes $68,000 a year)			
Snacks: Make snacks at home			
Alternate transportation: Walk, bicycle			
Work from home one or more days a week			
Take mass transit. It's not so bad!			
HOME ENERGY:			
Get free or low-cost solar panels:			
Reduce electricity bill by reducing inductive load			
Install attic fan to cool attic and reduce energy costs			
Use bed fan to cool bed at night ($100 savings per degree)			
Use space heater			
Use personal fan			
Insulate your house			
Eliminate drafts, close chimney flue, use weather stripping			
Install a programmable thermostat			
READING MATERIALS			
Get a Kindle to replace all the books magazines and newspapers I buy a year			
OTHER			
TOTAL			

A FEW MORE
Ideas On Some Changes.

I'm sure that was painful. But you must treat your finances like a business, and a business watches every penny that comes in and goes out. Yet with luck, you now have a target number you are comfortable meeting annually. I encourage you not to be too aggressive; start out small and grow into your ambitions. You will find that as you start becoming more aware of the things that you can do without in life, or make substitutions for, you will think of even more places to cut back. You may also start seeing a benefit in your health, which can sometimes be a big expense in itself.

When I was in college I would put a big calendar on the wall and record my daily expenses on the chart, drawing a star around those days when I spent nothing. We all need to feel rewarded, so don't forget to pat yourself on the back for achieving your goals.

Take a hard look at your spending records after a month or two. You'll be surprised when you look back at your record of expenses: $100 on books, $500 on gas… you'll likely see some obvious cuts you can make. Depending on how much you need to save, however, you may need to make

some difficult decisions. Think about your priorities and make cuts you can live with. Calculate how much those cuts will save you per year, and you'll be much more motivated to pinch pennies.

If you need a few more ideas on some changes you can make, here's a few simple ones.

Eliminate rote daily purchases.
These can really add up without your realizing it. Is the $3.50 coffee on your way to work absolutely necessary? At $1.50 each, how critical are the three sodas or snacks per day you buy from the office vending machine? A cup of coffee that you make at home costs only 25-35 cents. This kind of spending is mostly habitual and unnecessary, and saving money here is quick and easy. There will be some psychological pain at first, but when you add up the savings you'll feel a whole lot better.

Heating and cooling.
When you leave the house, set your thermostat to an "away" setting. But a note of caution: don't set it so far from comfortable that it takes an inordinate amount of energy to return the setting to normal

when you get home. In the winter, 65°F (18°C) is reasonable, and in the summer 80°F (27°C) is a handy setting to use. Consider investing in ceiling fans—you can get these for as little as $20 and they dramatically reduce the cost of heating and cooling by circulating air more efficiently. But adjust wisely: If your expenses are already low, and you won't be staying where you are for long, you may not save enough to pay for the fan.

Electric.

Lighting is expensive. When you leave a room, turn off the light. The idea that it takes more energy to turn on a light than to keep it on is completely false—it takes no more electricity to turn on a light than it does to keep it burning for a fraction of a second. Energy-efficient bulbs really work. This is a long-range investment that will pay off over time, but there is a significant savings to be gained. Also, turn off your computer or laptop when you're not using it—likely the only reason you leave it on is for convenience. And voltage adapters (including the ones in stereo components) still use electricity even if they're not charging or plugged into a device. If you have a digital box with an auxiliary AC outlet, plug your TV into it and program the box to shut off the outlet when the box is turned off. For stereo components, plug them all into a power strip that can easily be switched off when not in use. Further, open the drapes during the day for natural light instead of burning electricity. Rule of thumb: Only use electricity when you absolutely need it.

&A FEW MORE.

Water.

Save water, save money. Invest in a shower-reduction kit—it costs nearly nothing and will start saving you money immediately. Shower-reduction kits work by reducing water flow to the shower-head, and the change is barely noticeable. Learn to take quicker showers—an inexpensive egg timer is a good way to help. Repair leaky toilets and faucets, which are an enormous waste of water and easy to fix. Reduce your lawn-watering to minimum needs. If you have a pool, keep it covered when it's not in use to reduce evaporation; heating your pool also dramatically increases water evaporation. Only heat your pool to keep it from freezing, and invest in a thermal pool blanket. And if you're not using the water faucet, turn it off—as when brushing your teeth.

Gas and miscellaneous.

Do laundry as often as necessary but as little as possible. For a lot of people this is a pleasant step. Reduce the temperature of your shower by a few degrees; the less work your water heater does the more money you'll save. Use the microwave instead of the oven whenever possible—the cost to preheat an oven is more than the cost to cook a meal in the microwave. Open the windows when it's nice outside to reduce heating (and cooling) costs. If you live where natural gas is used only in the winter months, arrange with your local utility to do a seasonal shutoff so that you are not saddled with fixed monthly service charges for the "privilege" of being connected to the gas service, even though you're not using it. With one supplier, this privilege costs $17 a month. In the eight months that you don't need the service, you're charged $136. The season shutoff and turn-on costs only $54.

Reconsider gasoline, plus miscellaneous auto.

When gas was rationed during World War II, a popular slogan was, "Is this trip necessary?" Ask yourself this question every time you get in your car. Make a list before you go to the store so you don't have to make additional trips. Don't go for a pleasure drive—walk instead, or choose other forms of entertainment, such as reading or exercising. Check the pressure in your tires. Convertibles get better mileage with the top up. A poorly running engine is a huge waste of fuel—even a spark plug change can make a big difference, as can clean oil. Also, the less you drive the less frequently you'll change tires, oil, or require maintenance. That's a savings over time, of course, but it will mount up. Another way to save gas (and money) is to change your driving habits. By driving more slowly, and/or less aggressively, you can save significant amounts of money.

Coffee.

Invest in a good coffee machine. Making coffee at home instead of purchasing your $1, $3, or $4 custom latte at the coffee shop will save you money.

Lunch.

Consider taking your lunch to work instead of buying it each day. Even an inexpensive lunch out is several dollars a day—do the math.

Buy in bulk.

Look into joining a warehouse club. The price of the membership is usually made up in the first shopping trip. Bulk stores carry name-brand products and accept coupons. Also, buying in bulk lets you shop less often, so you not only save in-store but limit your commuting expenses to the store each week, as well as your exposure to the risk of impulse purchasing. Additionally, bulk purchases reduce your consumption of wasteful food packaging.

Consider pre-owned items.

This is a great way to save significant sums while recycling at the same time! If you absolutely must buy something, there are shopping options besides the mall anchor store or big-box superstore. Think of large thrift stores (e.g., Goodwill) or smaller church-run stores that have incredible bargains on everything from home knickknacks to appliances and clothing. It's amazing how fast a 4-year-old will outgrow shoes—and when he does, re-donate them so somebody else can benefit! Look for garage sales—your neighbors will definitely not think less of you because you bought that winter jacket they're trying to sell. Or hold your own garage sale—you never know who might want what you no longer need. And don't forget the bargains available at online sites like craigslist.org, freecycle.org, and ebay.com.

So Let's Start Putting Your Money To Work For YOU.

Given the crazy financial times right now, it might be a good idea to open an interest-bearing savings account. It's a lot easier to keep track of your savings if you keep them separate from your spending money. You can also usually get better interest on savings accounts than on checking accounts.

sure your accounts are FDIC-insured, and, if you're lucky enough to have saved more than $250,000, make sure that you have two social security numbers linked to each account. This is because each social security number at each financial institution is only insured up to $250,000.

More ambitious savers might consider higher-interest-bearing options such as CDs or money-market accounts for their longer-range savings goals. Regardless of the vehicle you choose, you should make

Pay yourself first.
This requires more effort than just tucking away whatever's leftover at the end of the month. Take charge of your savings goals. Deposit a predetermined sum into an account (or your piggy bank) as soon as you get

paid. An easy and effective way to start saving is to deposit 10% of every check into your savings account. If you get a check for, say, $610, move the decimal point one place to the left and deposit that amount: $61. This works well and requires little thought. In several years you'll find that you've amassed a tidy sum, and over decades you'll be a millionaire.

To get started, set up an automatic transfer from your checking account to your savings account. Many employers even let you to deduct money from your paycheck and deposit it directly into a savings account. It's so automatic that you never miss the money on your paycheck.

You can also have money deducted from your paycheck and deposited directly into a retirement account, with the taxes deferred until you withdraw the funds, which ideally will be when you retire. Retirement accounts are an excellent way to save for your future because of their built-in, tax-deferred advantages, as well as the fact that employers often match a portion your retirement contributions. In other words, free money! So if you have a 401(k), look to increase the amount that you're currently contributing.

Even if your employer doesn't match your retirement account contributions, try to maximize them to the legally permissible annual amount. And if you're already contributing the yearly maximum, consider opening an additional retirement

savings account, such as a Roth IRA, which possesses distinct tax-saving advantageous of its own, although on a different timetable.

The key to saving is to declare a predetermined amount of your regular earnings as untouchable, and then to put your savings plan on autopilot so you never have to think about it.

Overestimate your expenses and underestimate your income.

If you receive unexpected cash, put all or most of it into savings, but continue to set aside your regularly scheduled amount as well.

After a long week of working, you may want to indulge in some luxury, telling yourself, "I deserve this." But remember, the things you buy are not gifts to yourself: they are trades with your future. By exchanging products for money, you trade a piece of your present for a piece of your future.

To resist the impulse for immediate gratification, remind yourself about how smart and disciplined your are for keeping your eyes on the long-term prize.

And that nothing worth having ever comes easily.

It's all true.

Now Is A GREAT Time To Invest.

(Stocks are at historic lows).

We've all probably heard how it's a good idea to "make your money work for you." But what does this really mean? How can you make your money work for you? It's done, quite simply, by investing it.

We invest because it creates wealth by using the enormously powerful combination of compound interest and time.

Compound interest is a miracle.

Albert Einstein once remarked that the most powerful force in the universe is compound interest. It's amazing how quickly your money can grow when you earn interest on top of interest. At 10%, your money doubles every seven years.

Say you invest $100 per month in a mutual fund, at an annual rate of return of 11%. After 30 years, you will have put in a total of $36,000 in principal, but your investment will actually be worth about $280,450 because of compound interest. Investing $200 per month over the same time frame and at the same rate of return will yield about $561,000.

Consider an annual investment of $2,000:			
Years	Total invested	8% Return	10% Return
5	$10,000	$11,400	$12,210
15	$30,000	$54,300	$63,550
25	$50,000	$146,200	$196,700

Who can help you invest?

So how do you actually invest your money? You need to find a good broker. But choose carefully; brokers are paid on commission, so it's always in their best interest to make a transaction. Ultimately, you are responsible for your securing your financial future.

But don't be scared, just vigilant. Brokers come in three basic varieties.

Traditional broker.

Traditional brokers offer a wide range of services. They offer professional money-managers who will provide investment advice and help you allocate your money over different investment vehicles. Traditional brokerages make their money by charging for everything they do, and can cost more than other options.

Your financial institution.

Your bank probably has a financial planner who can assist you in outlining a

121

financial plan. They are often just tellers that have been promoted to this position. Still, it is a good way to get some free basic advice and, for the majority of us, it can be a good option. They may even have financial planners on staff who can help you make wise decisions at no charge.

Discount broker.

If you want to invest without professional assistance, a discount broker may be the way to go—especially if you are willing to do your own research and feel comfortable with your choices. They will charge you a small fee for making trades, but much less than if you had an expert do it for you. (If the company is Internet-based, the fees are even smaller.) You can have a lot of fun buying and selling stocks online, just be careful that you aren't spending all your time looking at your portfolio and making trades.

Monitor your portfolio.

Your life can change quite dramatically over your lifetime, and your investments should reflect your present and future situation. You may be able to be more aggressive early in your investment life, but want to take fewer risks toward the end of your investment horizon. Remember that saving and investing is for the long term: Expect setbacks, and view them not as failures but as investment lessons. Just be careful not to make the same mistake twice, otherwise your lesson will have gone for little.

Rich Hein/Sun-Times

You shouldn't feel intimidated about investing. This monkey, "Mr Monk," has beaten Wall Street four years in a row.

The financial world has a lot of jargon. I think much of it is meant to confuse and intimidate. "Derivatives," "warrants," "market caps." These are all simple concepts to understand if you invest the time.

The Different Kinds of Investment Tools

This may sound basic for some, but you'd be surprised how many people don't know the basics. Richard Branson, the multi-billionaire, didn't know the difference between net and gross until he was 50. So if you've heard any of this before, feel free to skip the sections you're already familiar with.

Cash equivalents.

Cash equivalents mean what they sound like— your money is just like cash. They are usually very low-risk. Interest rates are so low, however, so note that your investments here may not keep up with inflation. It's wise to keep only a portion of your savings in cash equivalents. These accounts are not designed to achieve your long-term growth objectives, but to offset risk in your other more aggressive investments. This is especially important right now.

Cash equivalents include:

Insured savings and checking accounts.

These accounts are a safe place to "park" your money, and are available at many different financial institutions, such as banks, credit unions, and savings and loans.

Money market accounts.

These are good if you have a larger balance and don't want to leave it in your checking account. They are for people who aren't going to want to access it often.

Money market funds.

These mutual funds invest only in short-term vehicles, such as Treasury bills, and CDs.

Certificates of Deposit (CDs).

If you don't mind keeping your money tied up for a few months, CDs are a great option, particularly now, when CDs are highly and the withdrawal terms so flexible. CDs are defined as short- or medium-term, interest-bearing, insured-debt instruments.

Bonds.

A bond is any security founded on debt. When you purchase a bond, you are lending your money to a company, state, or city for the construction of projects like roads, schools, or other large undertakings. Bond issuers pay you interest on your money, then pay you back your principal within a set amount of time.

Bonds are relatively safe investments. But this safety comes at a cost. Because they are low-risk, they also yield low returns. The rate of return on bonds is therefore generally lower than for other investment instruments.

What Could Possibly Go **Wrong?**

Some common pitfalls.

Before you run off and start throwing you money into a slew of investments, here are some things to consider first.

Even successful professionals make an occasional mistake when it comes to their investment strategy. Warren Buffet recently bought three billion dollars of General Electric, only to see its stock price tumble in a matter of weeks. While no one can foresee every issue down the road, there are a few mistakes you may successfully avoid with just a little forethought.

It's not planning to fail, but failing to plan.

The first bit of planning any investor should undertake is the development of the overall plan itself. Meeting with a financial advisor is the first step in establishing this plan. Interview an investment advisor like you would any employee. They will assess your current situation—usually for free—clearly identify your financial goals and objectives, and determine your personal risk comfort level. And investment plan is critical; without it, you risk becoming sidetracked, losing sight of your goals, or investing in ways inappropriate to your stage of life.

Expect the unexpected.

Planning for the unexpected is a great way to keep your investments headed in the right direction. Always keep an emergency fund of at least 5-6 months' worth of expenses on hand; this can ensure that financial hardship (like losing a job) will not ruin your long-term plans. Also, maintain sufficient insurance coverage. Insurance is a critical hedge against unexpected health problems, or even death. When the unexpected occurs, as it will, be prepared. You'd hate to have to surrender and reallocate the savings it took many years to accumulate.

Maximizing your plan.

You can't just put your money in five different stocks and forget about them. Since
the advent of the Dow Jones stock index in
1896, only one stock— General Electric—
still remains on the index today. So don't
expect much from those shares of U.S.
Leather Company you're still holding on to.

You must watch your portfolio and rebal-
ance it every few months to ensure you are
optimizing your assets. If you're waiting for
the DeLorean stock to bounce back, you
might be waiting awhile.

Don't wait until it's too late.

Creating an investment strategy is overwhelming, I know. And staying with it can
be even more difficult. Not surprisingly,
many people put off making investment
decisions because they're afraid of making
a bad choice, or feel that they don't understand it well enough. If you act sooner rather
than later, you will have the benefit of time
working for you.

Believe it or not, the investment strategy of
many people involves winning a lottery.

Getting a Little More
AGGRESSIVE.

Stocks.

When you purchase stocks (sometimes called equities), you become a part owner of the business. This entitles you to vote at the shareholders' meeting and allows you to receive dividends, which are derived from the profits that the company allocates to its stockholders. So if you own stock in Microsoft or Google, you actually own a piece of the company.

Stocks are volatile, that is, they fluctuate in value on a daily basis. We have seen more such volatility recently than in many decades. It's a good reminder that when you buy a stock there are absolutely no guarantees. It is common that the stocks of these companies don't even pay dividends, so the only way that your investment will grow is if the stock increases in value. If a company's stock value declines, you would then lose a portion of your investment. And if it goes out of business, then you might lose your entire investment.

Compared to bonds and other less aggressive investments, stocks can provide relatively high rates of return. Of course, there is a price for this upside: You must assume the risk of losing some or all of your investment.

My investment portfolio is managed by a very conservative financial advisor. And even so, it has lost a tremendous amount of value recently. So stocks are really for those who can afford to risk losing some of their funds.

There really aren't any blue chip stocks these days. Some of the most prestigious companies have hit tough times. But the good news is that there are bargains out there, with many stocks being undervalued currently.

Mutual funds.

Mutual funds work by pooling many thousands of investors' money to purchase a variety of bonds, cash equivalents, or stocks in order to meet certain investment objectives. Mutual funds have numerous advantages over picking your own stocks.

Professionally managed mutual funds are very diversified, which means that they are less risky than investing in a single stock. Management fees are baked into their cost. Also, it is not uncommon for some funds to charge a fee when they purchase or sell shares.

Currently, the worldwide value of all mutual funds totals more than $26 trillion, althought this number is likely to be significantly less after the recent plummeting of worldwide financial markets.

There are thousands of well-run mutual funds to choose from, however, with each

one highly focused on a given a market sector. Some mutual funds invest only in foreign companies and emerging markets, for example, while others concentrate on specific sectors, such as health care, transportation or technology.

Research before you buy.

It is extremely important to do your own research before you purchase any security. Even if you have an amazing broker, you need to feel comfortable and be able sleep at night. After all, it is your money, and never forget that your broker gets paid whether you win or lose. Don't fall for hot stock tips that promise to triple your money in three weeks. Save that behavior for Las Vegas.

Invest in green.

Right now, some of the best areas to invest in are the more socially responsible ones—specifically, those targeting green businesses, including anything from solar power to alternative fuels. Fair trade companies and companies that create sustainable products are also hot. These started out slowly but have quickly grown into the favorites of Wall Street, and if President Obama gets his way, this sector will grow to rival transportation and the pharmaceutical industry.

There are green mutual funds looking for green investors, and if you examine their recent stock prices you'll see that some of these funds actually did well when all else was crumbling around them. In my opinion, the best investment scenario is one in which you can make money and help the environment. This is also called voting with your wallet.

Get Rich SLOW.

We've all seen the schemes on TV to make millions overnight. The truth is that wealth accumulation is a marathon, not a sprint. And that anyone with the patience to become wealthy can do so.

A few years ago, when the dotcom companies went belly up, I lost a lot of money in the stock market. I told my financial advisor that the long term wasn't working out in the short term, and I pulled what was left of my money out of the market and put it in a savings account, where it earned a just a few percent interest.

If I had taken a longer view, and not overreacted to that situation, my account would be far better off today than it is now.

We are currently enduring the same kind of financial panic, and people think that they should pull all their money out of the market. But my own hard-won experience tells me that now is truly a great time to buy.

It's times like these when I'm reminded of that house I wish I had bought many years ago. The risk seemed too great at the time, but today its value is many times more than it was then.

Consider this: At a 10% rate of growth, your money will double every seven years, quadruple in fourteen years, and be eight times more valuable in a little over twenty years. That is a powerful argument for getting rich slow. And if you keep adding to that money as you go along, the amount you save can make you a millionaire.

Not everyone is ready for stocks right now, and that is understandable. If you fit this category, I would simply urge you not to lose your initiative to build wealth. There are great alternative investments available. What is your passion? Real estate? Starting a business? Go for it. Just keep in mind that building wealth is a long-term game, so check your dice at the door.

I have been fortunate to know some very wealthy business people across various fields. Billionaires, in fact. And they all had one thing in common: a passion for what they do. After they had made more money than they could spend in 10 lifetimes, and could afford to kick back and relax, they did just the opposite. They dived back into the same challenges that had made them wealthy in the first place. Why? Just because they loved it so much.

It seems the only thing better than wealth is having the right perspective on wealth.

Pay Yourself FIRST.

I want you to start visualizing the savings you have made. The problem with saving money is that the gains can seem abstract, and we often don't regard them the same way we might if they looked more like a shiny new grand piano.

Look at the checks on the following page. Then examine the forms alongside them. These forms represent the full magnitude of your Green Savings potential.

Our objective now is to become acutely aware of our spending in areas that have no effect on quality of life. In fact, I believe you are about to improve your quality of life by trimming spending. Carpooling, for example, is a great way to start the day. And eating less meat is healthier for you.

So have fun filling out these forms, and don't feel like it's a tax return. You will not be graded or judged. Without a doubt, though, you will begin to get a feel for the great improvements that small changes can make in your life.

January

THE BANK OF
THE GREEN MILLIONAIRE

Date _____

Pay to the Order of _____

Amount _____ $ [   ]

1234-3457-123456-123-1234 _____

February

THE BANK OF
THE GREEN MILLIONAIRE

Date _____

Pay to the Order of _____

Amount _____ $ [   ]

1234-3457-123456-123-1234 _____

March

THE BANK OF
THE GREEN MILLIONAIRE

Date _____

Pay to the Order of _____

Amount _____ $ [   ]

1234-3457-123456-123-1234 _____

An Example

Green Savings Areas	Before	This Month	Pay Yourself
Drinking filtered water from a reusable container	$90	$5	$85
Soda (vending machines, cans, bottles) or using a home soda maker	$63	$7	$56
Eliminating coffees cappucinos, lattes, etc., or using a cappcucino/coffee maker	$120	$20	$100
Carpooling, or not driving yourself to work	$220	$40	$180
Operating a second or third car Gas Insurance Maintainance Car payments Repairs Registration	$120 $100 $60 $240 $35 $230	$0	$785
Working from home Parking Tolls Snacks Gas Dry cleaning Clothes Coffee 25% cost of car	$110 $0 $90 $220 $35 $120 $70 $100	$25	$720
Home heating costs Turning down thermostat Using space heaters Blankets	$80	$50	$30
Insulating my house			
Using a Kindle instead of buying books Books Newspapers Magazines	$40	$10	$30
Changing all my light bulbs	$40	$20	$20
Properly inflating my tires Cost of gas a month (10% savings on fuel + tires)	$220	$198	$22
Using waste vegetable oil instead of gas Miles driven MPG of current car Cost of a gallon of gas Gas expense a month	$1200 22 $220 $190	$20	$170
Eating less meat Amount spent on steak, chicken, pork	$90	$20	$70
Getting free or greatly reduced solar panels Electricity utility			

The examples here have some duplication. For example, if you get rid of a car and work from home you will be saving the same money for the car expenses

Green Savings Areas	Before	This Month	Pay Yourself
Eliminating the standby mode on my home electronics (vampire energy)	$120	$105	$15
Installing a solar attic fan	$140	$120	$20
Cooling the house at night Using a bed fan to cool my bed at night	$100	$75	$25
Using a space heater	$100	$80	$20
Using a personal fan			
Installing a programmable thermostat	$110	$90	$20
Installing solar outdoor lighting	$20	$0	$20
Using rechargeable batteries	$10	$0	$10
Starting a home based business (the average one makes $68,000 a year)			
Bringing lunch to work in nonplastic lunch box	$140	$20	$120
Using fuel reformulator to reduce consumption and emissions	$190	$160	$30
Commuting by mass transit	$200	$20	$180
Composting waste food	$10	$0	$10
Getting Energy Star Refridgerator from Local Utility Co	$25	$15	$10
TOTAL	$3,928	$1,170	$2,758

This Month

THE BANK OF
THE GREEN MILLIONAIRE

Date 10/31/2009

Pay to the Order of Jane Jones

Amount Two Thousand S-even hundred fifty Eight XX/00

$ 2,758.00

1234-3457-123456-123-1234

Jane Jones

Green Savings Areas	Before	This Month	Pay Yourself
Drinking filtered water from a reusable container			
Soda (vending machines, cans, bottles) or using a home soda maker			
Eliminating coffees cappucinos, lattes, etc., or using a cappcucino/coffee maker			
Carpooling, or not driving yourself to work			
Operating a second or third car Gas Insurance Maintainance Car payments Repairs Registration			
Working from home Parking Tolls Snacks Gas Dry cleaning Clothes Coffee 25% cost of car			
Home heating costs Turning down thermostat Using space heaters Blankets			
Insulating my house			
Using a Kindle instead of buying books Books Newspapers Magazines			
Changing all my light bulbs			
Properly inflating my tires Cost of gas a month (10% savings on fuel + tires)			
Using waste vegetable oil instead of gas Miles driven MPG of current car Cost of a gallon of gas Gas expense a month			
Eating less meat Amount spent on steak, chicken, pork			
Getting free or greatly reduced solar panels Electricity utility			

The examples here have some duplication. For example, if you get rid of a car and work from home you will be saving the same money for the car expenses

Green Savings Areas	Before	This Month	Pay Yourself
Eliminating the standby mode on my home electronics (vampire energy)			
Installing a solar attic fan			
Cooling the house at night Using a bed fan to cool my bed at night			
Using a space heater			
Using a personal fan			
Installing a programmable thermostat			
Installing solar outdoor lighting			
Using rechargeable batteries			
Starting a home based business (the average one makes $68,000 a year)			
Bringing lunch to work in nonplastic lunch box			
Using fuel reformulator to reduce consumption and emissions			
Commuting by mass transit			
Composting waste food			
TOTAL			

January

THE BANK OF
THE GREEN MILLIONAIRE

Date

Pay to the Order of

Amount $

1234-3457-123456-123-1234

February

Green Savings Areas	Before	This Month	Pay Yourself
Drinking filtered water from a reusable container			
Soda (vending machines, cans, bottles) or using a home soda maker			
Eliminating coffees cappucinos, lattes, etc., or using a cappcucino/coffee maker			
Carpooling, or not driving yourself to work			
Operating a second or third car Gas Insurance Maintainance Car payments Repairs Registration			
Working from home Parking Tolls Snacks Gas Dry cleaning Clothes Coffee 25% cost of car			
Home heating costs Turning down thermostat Using space heaters Blankets			
Insulating my house			
Using a Kindle instead of buying books Books Newspapers Magazines			
Changing all my light bulbs			
Properly inflating my tires Cost of gas a month (10% savings on fuel + tires)			
Using waste vegetable oil instead of gas Miles driven MPG of current car Cost of a gallon of gas Gas expense a month			
Eating less meat Amount spent on steak, chicken, pork			
Getting free or greatly reduced solar panels Electricity utility			

The examples here have some duplication. For example, if you get rid of a car and work from home you will be saving the same money for the car expenses

Green Savings Areas	Before	This Month	Pay Yourself
Eliminating the standby mode on my home electronics (vampire energy)			
Installing a solar attic fan			
Cooling the house at night Using a bed fan to cool my bed at night			
Using a space heater			
Using a personal fan			
Installing a programmable thermostat			
Installing solar outdoor lighting			
Using rechargeable batteries			
Starting a home based business (the average one makes $68,000 a year)			
Bringing lunch to work in nonplastic lunch box			
Using fuel reformulator to reduce consumption and emissions			
Commuting by mass transit			
Composting waste food			
TOTAL			

February

THE BANK OF
THE GREEN MILLIONAIRE

Date _____

Pay to the Order of _____

Amount _____ $ _____

1234-3457-123456-123-1234

March

Green Savings Areas	Before	This Month	Pay Yourself
Drinking filtered water from a reusable container			
Soda (vending machines, cans, bottles) or using a home soda maker			
Eliminating coffees cappucinos, lattes, etc., or using a cappcucino/coffee maker			
Carpooling, or not driving yourself to work			
Operating a second or third car Gas Insurance Maintainance Car payments Repairs Registration			
Working from home Parking Tolls Snacks Gas Dry cleaning Clothes Coffee 25% cost of car			
Home heating costs Turning down thermostat Using space heaters Blankets			
Insulating my house			
Using a Kindle instead of buying books Books Newspapers Magazines			
Changing all my light bulbs			
Properly inflating my tires Cost of gas a month (10% savings on fuel + tires)			
Using waste vegetable oil instead of gas Miles driven MPG of current car Cost of a gallon of gas Gas expense a month			
Eating less meat Amount spent on steak, chicken, pork			
Getting free or greatly reduced solar panels Electricity utility			

The examples here have some duplication. For example, if you get rid of a car and work from home you will be saving the same money for the car expenses

Green Savings Areas	Before	This Month	Pay Yourself
Eliminating the standby mode on my home electronics (vampire energy)			
Installing a solar attic fan			
Cooling the house at night Using a bed fan to cool my bed at night			
Using a space heater			
Using a personal fan			
Installing a programmable thermostat			
Installing solar outdoor lighting			
Using rechargeable batteries			
Starting a home based business (the average one makes $68,000 a year)			
Bringing lunch to work in nonplastic lunch box			
Using fuel reformulator to reduce consumption and emissions			
Commuting by mass transit			
Composting waste food			
TOTAL			

March

THE BANK OF
THE GREEN MILLIONAIRE

Date _____

Pay to the Order of _____

Amount _____

$ [   ]

1234-3457-123456-123-1234

April

Green Savings Areas	Before	This Month	Pay Yourself
Drinking filtered water from a reusable container			
Soda (vending machines, cans, bottles) or using a home soda maker			
Eliminating coffees cappucinos, lattes, etc., or using a cappcucino/coffee maker			
Carpooling, or not driving yourself to work			
Operating a second or third car Gas Insurance Maintainance Car payments Repairs Registration			
Working from home Parking Tolls Snacks Gas Dry cleaning Clothes Coffee 25% cost of car			
Home heating costs Turning down thermostat Using space heaters Blankets			
Insulating my house			
Using a Kindle instead of buying books Books Newspapers Magazines			
Changing all my light bulbs			
Properly inflating my tires Cost of gas a month (10% savings on fuel + tires)			
Using waste vegetable oil instead of gas Miles driven MPG of current car Cost of a gallon of gas Gas expense a month			
Eating less meat Amount spent on steak, chicken, pork			
Getting free or greatly reduced solar panels Electricity utility			

The examples here have some duplication. For example, if you get rid of a car and work from home you will be saving the same money for the car expenses

Green Savings Areas	Before	This Month	Pay Yourself
Eliminating the standby mode on my home electronics (vampire energy)			
Installing a solar attic fan			
Cooling the house at night Using a bed fan to cool my bed at night			
Using a space heater			
Using a personal fan			
Installing a programmable thermostat			
Installing solar outdoor lighting			
Using rechargeable batteries			
Starting a home based business (the average one makes $68,000 a year)			
Bringing lunch to work in nonplastic lunch box			
Using fuel reformulator to reduce consumption and emissions			
Commuting by mass transit			
Composting waste food			
TOTAL			

April

THE BANK OF
THE GREEN MILLIONAIRE

Date _____

Pay to the Order of _____

Amount _____ $ [_____]

1234-3457-123456-123-1234 _____

May

Green Savings Areas	Before	This Month	Pay Yourself
Drinking filtered water from a reusable container			
Soda (vending machines, cans, bottles) or using a home soda maker			
Eliminating coffees cappucinos, lattes, etc., or using a cappcucino/coffee maker			
Carpooling, or not driving yourself to work			
Operating a second or third car Gas Insurance Maintainance Car payments Repairs Registration			
Working from home Parking Tolls Snacks Gas Dry cleaning Clothes Coffee 25% cost of car			
Home heating costs Turning down thermostat Using space heaters Blankets			
Insulating my house			
Using a Kindle instead of buying books Books Newspapers Magazines			
Changing all my light bulbs			
Properly inflating my tires Cost of gas a month (10% savings on fuel + tires)			
Using waste vegetable oil instead of gas Miles driven MPG of current car Cost of a gallon of gas Gas expense a month			
Eating less meat Amount spent on steak, chicken, pork			
Getting free or greatly reduced solar panels Electricity utility			

The examples here have some duplication. For example, if you get rid of a car and work from home you will be saving the same money for the car expenses

Green Savings Areas	Before	This Month	Pay Yourself
Eliminating the standby mode on my home electronics (vampire energy)			
Installing a solar attic fan			
Cooling the house at night Using a bed fan to cool my bed at night			
Using a space heater			
Using a personal fan			
Installing a programmable thermostat			
Installing solar outdoor lighting			
Using rechargeable batteries			
Starting a home based business (the average one makes $68,000 a year)			
Bringing lunch to work in nonplastic lunch box			
Using fuel reformulator to reduce consumption and emissions			
Commuting by mass transit			
Composting waste food			
TOTAL			

May

THE BANK OF
THE GREEN MILLIONAIRE

Date _____

Pay to the Order of _____

Amount _____ $ [   ]

1234-3457-123456-123-1234 _____

June

Green Savings Areas	Before	This Month	Pay Yourself
Drinking filtered water from a reusable container			
Soda (vending machines, cans, bottles) or using a home soda maker			
Eliminating coffees cappucinos, lattes, etc., or using a cappcucino/coffee maker			
Carpooling, or not driving yourself to work			
Operating a second or third car Gas Insurance Maintainance Car payments Repairs Registration			
Working from home Parking Tolls Snacks Gas Dry cleaning Clothes Coffee 25% cost of car			
Home heating costs Turning down thermostat Using space heaters Blankets			
Insulating my house			
Using a Kindle instead of buying books Books Newspapers Magazines			
Changing all my light bulbs			
Properly inflating my tires Cost of gas a month (10% savings on fuel + tires)			
Using waste vegetable oil instead of gas Miles driven MPG of current car Cost of a gallon of gas Gas expense a month			
Eating less meat Amount spent on steak, chicken, pork			
Getting free or greatly reduced solar panels Electricity utility			

The examples here have some duplication. For example, if you get rid of a car and work from home you will be saving the same money for the car expenses

Green Savings Areas	Before	This Month	Pay Yourself
Eliminating the standby mode on my home electronics (vampire energy)			
Installing a solar attic fan			
Cooling the house at night Using a bed fan to cool my bed at night			
Using a space heater			
Using a personal fan			
Installing a programmable thermostat			
Installing solar outdoor lighting			
Using rechargeable batteries			
Starting a home based business (the average one makes $68,000 a year)			
Bringing lunch to work in nonplastic lunch box			
Using fuel reformulator to reduce consumption and emissions			
Commuting by mass transit			
Composting waste food			
TOTAL			

June

THE BANK OF
THE GREEN MILLIONAIRE

Date _____

Pay to the Order of _____

Amount _____ $ _____

1234-3457-123456-123-1234 _____

July

Green Savings Areas	Before	This Month	Pay Yourself
Drinking filtered water from a reusable container			
Soda (vending machines, cans, bottles) or using a home soda maker			
Eliminating coffees cappucinos, lattes, etc., or using a cappcucino/coffee maker			
Carpooling, or not driving yourself to work			
Operating a second or third car Gas Insurance Maintainance Car payments Repairs Registration			
Working from home Parking Tolls Snacks Gas Dry cleaning Clothes Coffee 25% cost of car			
Home heating costs Turning down thermostat Using space heaters Blankets			
Insulating my house			
Using a Kindle instead of buying books Books Newspapers Magazines			
Changing all my light bulbs			
Properly inflating my tires Cost of gas a month (10% savings on fuel + tires)			
Using waste vegetable oil instead of gas Miles driven MPG of current car Cost of a gallon of gas Gas expense a month			
Eating less meat Amount spent on steak, chicken, pork			
Getting free or greatly reduced solar panels Electricity utility			

The examples here have some duplication. For example, if you get rid of a car and work from home you will be saving the same money for the car expenses

Green Savings Areas	Before	This Month	Pay Yourself
Eliminating the standby mode on my home electronics (vampire energy)			
Installing a solar attic fan			
Cooling the house at night Using a bed fan to cool my bed at night			
Using a space heater			
Using a personal fan			
Installing a programmable thermostat			
Installing solar outdoor lighting			
Using rechargeable batteries			
Starting a home based business (the average one makes $68,000 a year)			
Bringing lunch to work in nonplastic lunch box			
Using fuel reformulator to reduce consumption and emissions			
Commuting by mass transit			
Composting waste food			
TOTAL			

July

THE BANK OF
THE GREEN MILLIONAIRE

Date _____

Pay to the Order of _____

Amount _____ $ _____

1234-3457-123456-123-1234

August

Green Savings Areas	Before	This Month	Pay Yourself
Drinking filtered water from a reusable container			
Soda (vending machines, cans, bottles) or using a home soda maker			
Eliminating coffees cappucinos, lattes, etc., or using a cappcucino/coffee maker			
Carpooling, or not driving yourself to work			
Operating a second or third car Gas Insurance Maintainance Car payments Repairs Registration			
Working from home Parking Tolls Snacks Gas Dry cleaning Clothes Coffee 25% cost of car			
Home heating costs Turning down thermostat Using space heaters Blankets			
Insulating my house			
Using a Kindle instead of buying books Books Newspapers Magazines			
Changing all my light bulbs			
Properly inflating my tires Cost of gas a month (10% savings on fuel + tires)			
Using waste vegetable oil instead of gas Miles driven MPG of current car Cost of a gallon of gas Gas expense a month			
Eating less meat Amount spent on steak, chicken, pork			
Getting free or greatly reduced solar panels Electricity utility			

The examples here have some duplication. For example, if you get rid of a car and work from home you will be saving the same money for the car expenses

Green Savings Areas	Before	This Month	Pay Yourself
Eliminating the standby mode on my home electronics (vampire energy)			
Installing a solar attic fan			
Cooling the house at night Using a bed fan to cool my bed at night			
Using a space heater			
Using a personal fan			
Installing a programmable thermostat			
Installing solar outdoor lighting			
Using rechargeable batteries			
Starting a home based business (the average one makes $68,000 a year)			
Bringing lunch to work in nonplastic lunch box			
Using fuel reformulator to reduce consumption and emissions			
Commuting by mass transit			
Composting waste food			
TOTAL			

August

THE BANK OF
THE GREEN MILLIONAIRE

Date _____

Pay to the Order of _____

Amount _____ $ [   ]

1234-3457-123456-123-1234   _____

September

Green Savings Areas	Before	This Month	Pay Yourself
Drinking filtered water from a reusable container			
Soda (vending machines, cans, bottles) or using a home soda maker			
Eliminating coffees cappucinos, lattes, etc., or using a cappcucino/coffee maker			
Carpooling, or not driving yourself to work			
Operating a second or third car Gas Insurance Maintainance Car payments Repairs Registration			
Working from home Parking Tolls Snacks Gas Dry cleaning Clothes Coffee 25% cost of car			
Home heating costs Turning down thermostat Using space heaters Blankets			
Insulating my house			
Using a Kindle instead of buying books Books Newspapers Magazines			
Changing all my light bulbs			
Properly inflating my tires Cost of gas a month (10% savings on fuel + tires)			
Using waste vegetable oil instead of gas Miles driven MPG of current car Cost of a gallon of gas Gas expense a month			
Eating less meat Amount spent on steak, chicken, pork			
Getting free or greatly reduced solar panels Electricity utility			

The examples here have some duplication. For example, if you get rid of a car and work from home you will be saving the same money for the car expenses

Green Savings Areas	Before	This Month	Pay Yourself
Eliminating the standby mode on my home electronics (vampire energy)			
Installing a solar attic fan			
Cooling the house at night Using a bed fan to cool my bed at night			
Using a space heater			
Using a personal fan			
Installing a programmable thermostat			
Installing solar outdoor lighting			
Using rechargeable batteries			
Starting a home based business (the average one makes $68,000 a year)			
Bringing lunch to work in nonplastic lunch box			
Using fuel reformulator to reduce consumption and emissions			
Commuting by mass transit			
Composting waste food			
TOTAL			

September

THE BANK OF
THE GREEN MILLIONAIRE

Date _____

Pay to the Order of _____

Amount _____ $ [   ]

1234-3457-123456-123-1234

October

Green Savings Areas	Before	This Month	Pay Yourself
Drinking filtered water from a reusable container			
Soda (vending machines, cans, bottles) or using a home soda maker			
Eliminating coffees cappucinos, lattes, etc., or using a cappcucino/coffee maker			
Carpooling, or not driving yourself to work			
Operating a second or third car Gas Insurance Maintainance Car payments Repairs Registration			
Working from home Parking Tolls Snacks Gas Dry cleaning Clothes Coffee 25% cost of car			
Home heating costs Turning down thermostat Using space heaters Blankets			
Insulating my house			
Using a Kindle instead of buying books Books Newspapers Magazines			
Changing all my light bulbs			
Properly inflating my tires Cost of gas a month (10% savings on fuel + tires)			
Using waste vegetable oil instead of gas Miles driven MPG of current car Cost of a gallon of gas Gas expense a month			
Eating less meat Amount spent on steak, chicken, pork			
Getting free or greatly reduced solar panels Electricity utility			

The examples here have some duplication. For example, if you get rid of a car and work from home you will be saving the same money for the car expenses

Green Savings Areas	Before	This Month	Pay Yourself
Eliminating the standby mode on my home electronics (vampire energy)			
Installing a solar attic fan			
Cooling the house at night Using a bed fan to cool my bed at night			
Using a space heater			
Using a personal fan			
Installing a programmable thermostat			
Installing solar outdoor lighting			
Using rechargeable batteries			
Starting a home based business (the average one makes $68,000 a year)			
Bringing lunch to work in nonplastic lunch box			
Using fuel reformulator to reduce consumption and emissions			
Commuting by mass transit			
Composting waste food			
TOTAL			

October

November

Green Savings Areas	Before	This Month	Pay Yourself
Drinking filtered water from a reusable container			
Soda (vending machines, cans, bottles) or using a home soda maker			
Eliminating coffees cappucinos, lattes, etc., or using a cappcucino/coffee maker			
Carpooling, or not driving yourself to work			
Operating a second or third car Gas Insurance Maintainance Car payments Repairs Registration			
Working from home Parking Tolls Snacks Gas Dry cleaning Clothes Coffee 25% cost of car			
Home heating costs Turning down thermostat Using space heaters Blankets			
Insulating my house			
Using a Kindle instead of buying books Books Newspapers Magazines			
Changing all my light bulbs			
Properly inflating my tires Cost of gas a month (10% savings on fuel + tires)			
Using waste vegetable oil instead of gas Miles driven MPG of current car Cost of a gallon of gas Gas expense a month			
Eating less meat Amount spent on steak, chicken, pork			
Getting free or greatly reduced solar panels Electricity utility			

The examples here have some duplication. For example, if you get rid of a car and work from home you will be saving the same money for the car expenses

Green Savings Areas	Before	This Month	Pay Yourself
Eliminating the standby mode on my home electronics (vampire energy)			
Installing a solar attic fan			
Cooling the house at night Using a bed fan to cool my bed at night			
Using a space heater			
Using a personal fan			
Installing a programmable thermostat			
Installing solar outdoor lighting			
Using rechargeable batteries			
Starting a home based business (the average one makes $68,000 a year)			
Bringing lunch to work in nonplastic lunch box			
Using fuel reformulator to reduce consumption and emissions			
Commuting by mass transit			
Composting waste food			
TOTAL			

November

THE BANK OF
THE GREEN MILLIONAIRE

Date

Pay to the Order of

Amount $

1234-3457-123456-123-1234

December

Green Savings Areas	Before	This Month	Pay Yourself
Drinking filtered water from a reusable container			
Soda (vending machines, cans, bottles) or using a home soda maker			
Eliminating coffees cappucinos, lattes, etc., or using a cappcucino/coffee maker			
Carpooling, or not driving yourself to work			
Operating a second or third car Gas Insurance Maintainance Car payments Repairs Registration			
Working from home Parking Tolls Snacks Gas Dry cleaning Clothes Coffee 25% cost of car			
Home heating costs Turning down thermostat Using space heaters Blankets			
Insulating my house			
Using a Kindle instead of buying books Books Newspapers Magazines			
Changing all my light bulbs			
Properly inflating my tires Cost of gas a month (10% savings on fuel + tires)			
Using waste vegetable oil instead of gas Miles driven MPG of current car Cost of a gallon of gas Gas expense a month			
Eating less meat Amount spent on steak, chicken, pork			
Getting free or greatly reduced solar panels Electricity utility			

157   The examples here have some duplication. For example, if you get rid of a car and work from home you will be saving the same money for the car expenses

Green Savings Areas	Before	This Month	Pay Yourself
Eliminating the standby mode on my home electronics (vampire energy)			
Installing a solar attic fan			
Cooling the house at night Using a bed fan to cool my bed at night			
Using a space heater			
Using a personal fan			
Installing a programmable thermostat			
Installing solar outdoor lighting			
Using rechargeable batteries			
Starting a home based business (the average one makes $68,000 a year)			
Bringing lunch to work in nonplastic lunch box			
Using fuel reformulator to reduce consumption and emissions			
Commuting by mass transit			
Composting waste food			
TOTAL			

December

THE BANK OF
THE GREEN MILLIONAIRE

Date

Pay to the Order of

Amount

$

1234-3457-123456-123-1234